11 Easy Steps to Raise a Brat

11 Easy Steps to Raise a Brat

♦

Paying Attention to Your Parenting Decisions Even When Life Is Too Busy to Pay Attention—It Matters.

Deborah M. Boccanfuso

iUniverse, Inc.
New York Lincoln Shanghai

11 Easy Steps to Raise a Brat

Paying Attention to Your Parenting Decisions Even When Life Is Too Busy to Pay Attention—It Matters.

All Rights Reserved © 2004 by Deborah M. Boccanfuso

No part of this book may be reproduced or transmitted in any form or by any means, graphic, electronic, or mechanical, including photocopying, recording, taping, or by any information storage retrieval system, without the written permission of the publisher.

iUniverse, Inc.

For information address:
iUniverse, Inc.
2021 Pine Lake Road, Suite 100
Lincoln, NE 68512
www.iuniverse.com

ISBN: 0-595-31638-7 (pbk)
ISBN: 0-595-66352-4 (cloth)

Printed in the United States of America

Many Thanks.

I wish to thank Stephanie, Melissa, Kevin, and Vincent for being "my brats" who
inspire me every day to ask "Will it matter in 10 years?"
and Vinnie for his continuous support and love
regardless of how many crazy dreams I can come up with.
A special thanks to Mary and Charlie Keller, my parents,
for being great roles models for me,
and to Leslie, Lisa, Danny, my friends, family members,
colleagues, and the parents I interact with every day.
Thanks for helping me keep life in perspective
and focused on what really matters.

Contents

Foreword

I like to think of this book as a culmination of the numerous presentations and hundreds of conversations I've had with individual parents over the past eighteen years as a public school employee. My degrees in special education, regular education, administration, and doctoral candidacy in educational leadership gave me the "book knowledge" for this book, but life experiences have been the real inspiration for *11 Easy Steps to Raise a Brat*.

I never thought my career would keep me entrenched in the adolescent world, yet it has. And I am forever grateful for that fact. Often I serve as a translator for adolescents as they try to communicate to their parents. On other occasions I am the interpreter for the parent whose adolescent just can't understand what his parent is talking about. In either role, I watch and think about each individual and the interactions that they share with me.

My experiences have made me somewhat of an expert in the realm of raising children. I've worked with thousands of kids—tall, short, fat, skinny, handsome, awkward, kind, mean, talented, clumsy, well behaved, and bratty. I've seen hundreds of parents try to figure their children out. The process is the same for all parent-child relationships. We can debate the nature versus nurture influences until the world stops spinning. And, suffice it to say, on any given day, I may sit on either side of the fence depending upon the argument at hand. However, my experiences tell me that parents are extremely influential in their child's ultimate ability to cope, grow, learn, and fit into our societal norms. We, as parents, have tremendous power. In the face of a comprehensive and complex world, we need to use this power productively. It is my firm belief that we have to start productively raising our children at a very early age, perhaps two, instead of twelve years old.

This book is a conglomeration of ideas. I've tried to break it into five interrelated parts, even though I have been advised to break it into five separate, expanded books. I appreciated that advice and thought about it long and hard. But then I realized, as a working mother, it is often better for me to have one book and pick and choose the parts I read at different times. Therefore, I decided to keep it as one book with five distinct but related parts. You can be the judge. Read it all at once or save parts for different times in your parenting life. It's fine with me either way. I just want you to enjoy the book and think deeply about your commitment to raising healthy and socially competent children. Always be vigilant of your goals for raising your children. It is very easy to fall into the trap of the 11 easy steps to raise a brat. Enjoy.

Love, Debi Boccanfuso—August 2004

My Assumptions

Parenting doesn't start when your child is twelve. Honestly, it starts way before he is even two. That's a long time before the adolescent spirit emerges to test all your fabulous parenting techniques. You are just another step along the generational chain of raising children. Some kids end up fine; others end up as brats.

Every generation believes it is faced with the most challenging parenting issues. Our generation is no different. The truth is there have always been parenting issues. I would venture to say that every one of us has a grandparent somewhere on our family tree that starts every sentence with, "Back when I was raising my kids…" and then reveals the big issues of her time. From our grandparents' mouths come the introductions and parenting fears of teen sex, drugs, and rock-n-roll. These pearls of wisdom from our elders may be true, but it doesn't make our issues and parenting decisions today any less valid. Over the past forty years, parents have seen their children turn to alcohol and drugs to help cope with the demands and hectic pace of today's world. Sexually transmitted diseases are now talked about in schools with our ten-year olds. Many of them may not even know what their bodies are capable of, but now they do know they can catch all kinds of diseases. And, almost anything goes with regard to music lyrics. We now have ratings on our movies, TV shows, video games, and music compact discs to try to help parents understand the bombardment of "stuff" they need to deal with as parents of the 21st century. Our grandparents wouldn't have been able to imagine what is out there now.

The fact is, parenting has never been easy, and every generation has had its own story to tell. All generations have had their specific parenting issues to deal with. Their parenting decisions were handled as they tried to filter information and manipulate their environments to try their best to produce healthy offspring who could cope with life. Our generation is no different. The game of raising children has not changed; some of the rules, though, are now possibly more challenging.

We now live in a hectic, busy, and complex world. Many of us work outside of our homes to make ends meet and provide for our family. While we are at work, we worry about our children at home or at school. When we are home with our family, we try to fit everything in and provide our family with experiences, opportunities, and traditions. Some of us deal with this crazy multi-tasking quite well. Some of us lay way too much guilt on ourselves when our efforts start to crumble. And, some of us get so overwhelmed with the task of parenting that we want to throw in the towel.

But don't. There is hope. As long as you can filter the information that is out there about raising children, seek the necessary skills and apply them to your day-to-day parenting decisions, there is a great possibility that a healthy adult will be produced from your home. An adult who can balance a professional and personal life, manage stress, and develop strong interpersonal relationships should be the goal of every parenting experience. Our parenting decisions start as soon as this future adult takes his first breath as a newborn. This goal can not happen without forethought and planning, quality decision-making, patience and boundaries, love and support. These ingredients are essential and, at times, needed in dispro-portionate amounts.

My wholehearted belief is that to raise a great kid takes a lot of important short-term decisions and actions with a firm, grounded long-term plan. If you are not focusing your goals on "a great kid or adult who can cope with life," the end result could be "a brat who seems to never grow up." Be careful. Parenting today is not easy. How you handle it all now will have a huge impact on your child's overall development and coping skills later in his life.

My research for this book comes from first-hand experiences of being a middle school educator and administrator in the public school system. My professional witness of hundreds of parent-child interactions gives testimony to the awesome task of managing the parental issues of today's complex world. With my own family and career, I am living in the moment with you. I am sure someday my statements will begin with, "Back when I was raising my kids…"

Will It Matter in Ten Years?

For many years people have said to me, "How do you do it?" What they are referring to is what millions of people do everyday—work and raise a family. I never thought I was doing anything differently than anyone else, but after several years of the same questions and more and more people telling me what "nice kids I had," I gave it some serious thought and realized something important. It wasn't that I was doing anything mysterious while raising my children. I had no magic wand. I did realize, however, I had been using a filtering question for almost every decision I made when dealing with my children, "Will it matter in ten years?" If the answer was no, I wouldn't spend much time on the issue. However, if the answer was yes, it was worth the battle; a battle I don't mind.

Parenting is a profession that no one is completely (or sometimes even remotely) prepared for when they enter it. Armed only with the skills and beliefs we've learned through our parents (for better or for worse), we are off and running the minute that tiny breath is taken and the wailing begins in the labor room. It has astonished me over the years how resilient kids are at times, and how unknowing some parents can be, at times.

As parents, sometimes we get worked up over things that don't matter and at other times we are too relaxed about things that really should matter. Sometimes it is hard to determine the short-term-doesn't-matter issues from the long-term-really-does-matter issues and vice versa. The question, "Will it matter in ten years?" needs to be asked continuously because as your child's needs, desires, and capabilities change, so might the answers to this central question change.

I do, however, remain firm in the fact that some global issues will never change regardless of the age of our children or when we decide to ask the question. These include issues around respect, trust, commitment, self-advocacy skills, and good communication skills. But, I know fully well that some issues will absolutely change depending on the age of our children and the timing of when we ask ourselves that vital question. These issues include things like rules, expectations, friendships, relationships, and desires.

At times, very honestly, parents may need to seek professional assistance from a counselor, therapist, or psychologist depending upon the magnitude of the issues they deal with. But, I do believe this is exactly why the question must remain constant as time ticks by. Parents need a framework to work within so that they can be consistent with their child in this inconsistent state of "growing up," and so they can assess their child's needs on a regular basis. How else can parents know that the issues are bigger than what they can handle if they haven't been monitoring these daily decisions and battles as they arise, with some fundamental guiding tool? This question, "Will it matter in ten years?" can be a parent's beacon to guide them through a potentially tumultuous journey of parenting.

My professional life has added another level to my parenting technique and strategies. I was a teacher, an assistant principal, and now a principal at a middle school of a thousand students. These roles have allowed me to experience first hand hundreds of parent/child interactions—some good, some bad, some sad, even pathetic, and some outstanding. Regardless of the outcome, the individuals involved always taught me something. I've tried to incorporate my experiences into this book and synthesize them into manageable pieces.

In this book I may sound sarcastic and direct at times. I make no apologies for that. My humorous moments will be shared from time to time. My personal moments with my children are out there for the world to see. Not always the winner of a Perfect Parenting Award, my experiences and reflections are here to be used as examples. Embedded in it all are my thoughts. Some may seem profound and some not. Sometimes I may sound like an expert and sometimes not. Whichever the case may be, I do believe the sincerity behind it all will shine through.

As I wrote in the foreword, this book has five parts. Some may be more important to you than others, but in fairness I will give you my rationale for each.

"Part I: 11 Easy Steps to Raise A Brat," is based on the premise that it is truly unbelievably easy to raise a brat. Many parents are doing it every day. We know these brats by their fresh mouths, their need for immediate attention from adults and peers, or the parents' pride as their child wreaks havoc on the school playground. This chapter title is somewhat sarcastic in nature, but points out the incredibly important lifelong societal rules children learn by the parenting decisions we can make each day using the filter, "Will it matter in ten years?" Each step, within Part I, elaborates the consequences and messages, both spoken and unspoken, that are sent through our actions and inactions. We need to be careful of the messages embedded in our parenting decisions that we send all the time.

"Part II: The Great Adventure: The Parent-Teacher Conference" focuses on how parents can have productive conferences with their child's teacher to gain insights into their child's education. I've included this chapter in the book because children will spend more waking hours with teachers and peers they hardly know than with their own family members. That's a reality for all parents, not just working parents who don't have the option of home-schooling their children. This is an important relationship that needs to be fostered and nurtured by each side. Either partner in the relationship, parent or teacher, could "blow it" if the relationship is not attended to. The question, "Will it matter in ten years?" is a filter by which parents can choose to share information or decide how to react to receiving information throughout the many parent-teacher conferences parents will have regarding their child's education.

"Part III: A Middle School Kid Moved In Last Night" was included for two reasons. First, babies turn into adolescents before we know it, and for the vast majority out there, they will continue to live in your home during their adolescent years. Second, it is in the adolescent world that I have chosen to spend my entire professional life. Therefore, I chose to include it. I am passionate and intrigued by this age child. To me early adolescence is a myriad of parts working hard to come together—a kaleidoscope of body parts and emotions mixed together with some raging hormones. Just like unique fingerprints, no two early adolescents are ever the same. What a powerful thought. For most parents it is a terrifying time. The angel they put to bed one night wakes up the next day as an ugly monster who speaks but often seems to make no sense. Sometimes this transformation literally seems to happen overnight. In my dealings with hundreds of parents, many of my conversations come back to what the early adolescent needs in order to "make it through" and what the parents need to "get their child, and themselves, through" this period of time. Therefore, this part of the book is hopefully one of enlightenment and awareness about adolescents for most readers. (Good luck.)

"Part IV: The Big Scary World" seemed to be a natural flow from Part III. If this "creature" evolves and now lives in your house, it can only help to understand the daunting environment one must become familiar with. At a certain point, parents may want to become intimately familiar with various aspects I will point out, but for now, in Part IV, I have offered just an overview. Parents tell me they can't stand their kids' music so they turn off their kids' favorite radio station when they are alone in the car, or they leave the room if the kids want to watch their TV shows. I beg parents to listen to the "cool station" when they are alone in the car, pop in their kids' CDs, or watch what they are watching on the TV. Parents need to stay in tune with what their children are bombarded with. This section highlights only ten "scary world" concepts, but there are dozens more; maybe even hundreds. The ones included are not in any order, nor are they heavily documented with empirical research. They are, however, there to open minds, spark a conversation, and raise awareness. Every one of these concepts matters now, and/or potentially will have a great impact on our child in ten years.

"Part V: It's Just an Illusion: Making the Working Mom Thing Look Easy" is my gift to everyday parents. It is my personal favorite. Dads are invited to read this chapter as well, but it has been written from my point of view—a working mother's point of view. Working mothers who dream of doing the best for their children, must ask themselves, "Will it matter in ten years for me?" They must not lose themselves while raising their children. Yes, parents need to sacrifice some things and delete some personal time from their schedule, but they should guard against losing themselves and forgetting that when their children grow up, become taxpayers, and leave the house, they themselves will need personal interests, hobbies, skills, friendships, and their own personal relationships. They shouldn't have to start from scratch, if they've nurtured their own spirit along the way. This section is meant to give parents strategies to help them manage time and organize their kids' lives and their own lives so that there is time to continue to do the things they love. Readers can use some of these ideas in Part V or throw them all out and create their own. Parents should ask, "Will what I am doing with my time and energy matter in ten years to me?" The answer may be surprising.

So now, "Will it matter in ten years?" We, as parents, have made the choice of taking on the incredible responsibility of raising our future. These children come to us with no manuals. Our mentors may be just as inexperienced as we are. Although our skills have been shaped and reinforced by our own parents, our jobs as parents are becoming more complicated as the world gets smaller and more complex. The Internet, music videos, scheduled sports programs, movies, and economic issues have all impacted our child-rearing in ways that were not an issue for our parents.

This book is full of advice, professional experiences and insights, and my personal examples. Some pieces of advice you will like and other pieces you will hate. Either way, it is fine with me. This book is about your decisions, not mine. Take what you like and leave the rest. That is your personal choice.

There is one vital piece of advice I must give before you read any further, though. Please try not to ignore this one. Try your best to get to know the parents of your child's friends. There are not enough hours in a day for you to get to know everyone your child will befriend. Therefore, you must network. Take the time (although that may seem impossible) to get together to talk, drink wine or tea, and laugh with your own peers so that you can get a sense of what's going on in your child's world. (P.S. This time dedicated to being with other adults also gives your child the illusion that you know everyone.) My Republican dad would hate to admit this, but perhaps Hillary Clinton was right when she titled her book, *It Takes A Village*. We all are a part of an incredible village capable of helping each other raise our children. Try your best to know who is in your child's village.

I have already provided you with a synopsis of each of the ensuing chapters. They are meant to be thought-provoking, inspiring, and challenging. Read them with an open mind. Refer back to your own parents' parenting skills. Contemplate your family's values and what type of child or teenager you want living in your house and functioning in society. Listen to the words. Listen to your heart. Know and feel the love you have for your own child.

I know and can appreciate that advice is always easier said than done. I also know that the decisions you make may or may not be influenced by this book, but if nothing else, the next time you have to address a behavior with your child you may just pause to think, "Will it matter in ten years?"

Part I:

11 Easy Steps to Raise a Brat

Raising a brat is quite an easy job. Living with a brat for the rest of one's life can be quite a challenge, though. Raising brats is easy; just say yes all the time. Let the brat do whatever he wants—always. Why stifle his cute creative interests, even if it oversteps some boundaries? Go ahead and work around the kid's agenda. A brat will emerge, develop, and become a fairly self-centered individual.

There are very real benefits to raising a brat. It is easier in the short-term, although a potential nightmare in the long-run. Raising a brat is a whole lot more fun initially. You can be his best friend and number one fan every day. This can be cute because a child with a precocious nature can be considered "inquisitive" and "chatty." Be careful. This same child can sometimes be interpreted as rude by those who are inundated with the precocious cutie-pie.

The term "brat" may sound a bit harsh to some people, so let me give a definition for the term. I define "brat" as one who has learned that it is acceptable to disregard the needs and desires of others, and puts *his* needs, interests, and desires first on a regular and predictable basis. The average person may recognize a brat by some general characteristics: selfish, unable to put his own needs on hold, blurts out statements whenever the feeling arises—regardless of the appropriateness, demanding of others, and determined to gain the majority of the attention of those in his/her presence.

Brats don't hatch from eggs, nor are they dropped onto Mother Earth. They are nurtured, supported, and loved by parents who believe it is too hard to say *no*, or who are, perhaps, afraid to stifle their child's imagination or creativity by having him conform to generally accepted social norms. These loving parents satisfy their baby's needs with only the short-term in mind. The reality is that every decision made today affects the long-term development of a child. The toughest part of raising a child who is able to cope with life's challenges is keeping the balance between short-term desire and behavior with long-term social goals for your child—ten years from now.

The time to lay the foundation to nurture a caring, well-rounded adolescent starts very early. Babies and toddlers learn at a pace that amazes us. Their world is one of trial and error. Repetition and boundaries create a predictable and safe environment for learning appropriate social behaviors. They learn every minute of every day. And, they test the limits of their loving parents. With all the risks and challenges and opportunities they will face, our goal as parents should be to raise a child who can grow into an adult capable of coping with whatever life throws at them.

Buckle up. Its' a wonderful roller coaster ride. We may not always be in the driver's seat, but the more times we are, the better chance we'll have at steering our children in the right direction.

The goal is honorable. The challenge is awesome. Raise a solid, capable kid or go for the brat. *The choice is ours.*

The following offers guidance down the path to raising the perfect brat in 11 easy steps. Enjoy.

STEP 1—BUY THEM ANYTHING THEY WANT

The toy store—a parent's nightmare. A tired, overworked mom (or dad) grits their teeth and steams, "Cut it out." at their child in a toy store and then complains aloud to almost anyone, "I can't believe this kid. He wants everything here."

No kidding? I have two feelings about this: One, don't bring the kids into the toy store; two, deal with it—after all, the parent brought the child there. As far as I know the driving age is not four years old, so she did not come alone.

One step beyond the tired, overworked, cranky parent is "the negotiator." You can recognize the "negotiators" when you hear them saying to their children, "If you are good, and stop the whining, you can pick out one thing before we leave." What lesson is here for that child? Whine, then stop, and get his way anyway. Instant gratification at it's best!

Materialism abounds us. It is a part of our world. Material objects are sometimes used to fulfill the emotional need of the child or the feelings of guilt on the part of the parent. Remember, nothing replaces the long-term benefits of love, time, and energy. Frequently, material objects just simply overshadow the short-term feelings of guilt, lack of energy, or just plain tiredness. Be cautious of the setting that you set up for yourself and your child. The parent has a choice of how to deal with the toy store scene—or any situation that is similar in nature.

Our children are growing up in a world of materialism and instant gratification. The impact may perplex us all. Microwaves, computer programs and technology, one hundred channels on TV, and music downloading capabilities are just a few of the things that are instantly available to our children. It's not their fault that their demands can be met instantly. Life as we knew it has changed. However, our role, with regard to their expectations of the world, can make a difference to our children.

Instead of instantly "buying anything they want" whenever they want, there are important lessons every child must learn to become a productive adult in society. In addition to delayed gratification, they must learn the concept of patience. Children who demand, and consistently and quickly gain their desired material objects through their demands, are not learning that patience and postponed gratification are often a part of life. It would be nice, as adults, to have everything we want instantly, on demand; however, that is not how the world works. We typically work all week and get paid at the end. We usually do not go into the car dealership to buy a car and drive it out in ten minutes, even though we may need it (or want it) immediately. I admit, even as adults, instant loan acceptances, ATMs, microwaves, and cell phones continue to create and foster a lifestyle of instant gratification. However, the lesson our children need to learn is that hard work, patience, and postponed gratification are important parts of life if personal gain is the desired outcome. Just remember, there is no law that says "All parents must buy everything their children want." The real choice to do so is ours.

Guiding question 1 might be: "In ten years, will my child be able to have the patience to work hard and delay his gratification so that he may receive what he truly needs, not just what he wants?"

STEP 2—NEVER SAY NO

One day, while watching Oprah, my daughter, who was nine years old at the time, and I sat in silence as "out of control teenage daughters" told off their mothers on national TV. One mother sat there and cried, saying that she found it so hard to say no to her daughter. My daughter Stephanie turned to me and said, "You have no problem in that department; that's for sure."

She was right. "No" is a common word in my house, and I see its value and life lessons as I frequently say it.

I stopped getting a familiar parenting magazine the day the cover titles were, "Never say NO," "Give your child choices," and "Learning to live with the guilt." I couldn't take it any more. It was almost inferred that by saying no, parents were somehow damaging their children and limiting their experiences. I see *no* in a very different way. To me, saying *no* allows children to learn limits. It sets boundaries that they cannot set for themselves when they are young. It delays gratification in many instances, and sometimes can bring satisfaction in uncertain situations. It can bring safety to an impulsive child and can set the record straight for a child who is feeling out of control. Saying *no* helps a child learn how to handle frustration and grow from uncomfortable situations. Saying *no* helps children prioritize their needs and separate them from their wants. Saying *no* is necessary in raising a good, stable child in today's complex world. It is my firm belief that all children (and adolescents, especially) feel safer when there are clear boundaries in place.

I often wonder why so many parents have such a hard time saying no to their children. Perhaps it is because they work and feel guilty because there are so many times they can't be with their children, so they don't want to disappoint them one more time by saying no to them. Perhaps it's because they can afford the material things that their children want (and kids always want something), so why should their children go without, when it is within the realm of financial possibilities? Perhaps it's because parents are afraid of their children's rejection and hatred (*please* see step 11). Or, perhaps, they haven't realized that sometimes no builds character and that the child will live through the trauma of the word *no*. Remember, as long as a child is well fed, has clothes on her back, has a roof over her head, and has her parents' love, *no* will not harm her.

Emotionally, we have to be strong enough to handle the no's we will have to give over and over. At age two, *no* seems traumatic (No, you can't go into the water right now). At age seven, *no* seems inconvenient (No, you cannot go over to Johnny's until I talk to his mom). At age twelve, *no* may have high stakes attached to it (*No.* You cannot go to the girl/boy party with no chaperones). Yes, we may be the geeky parent who has too many rules, but remember, as long as our children are well fed, have clothes on their backs, have a roof overhead, and have our love, *no* will not harm them.

Guiding question 2 might be: "In ten years, will the no *matter?"*

STEP 3—EXPECT NO MANNERS—LET 'EM BURP

One day, while at Burger King, two kids at the table across from ours were being quite rude. All right, they were only about four or five years old, so "rude" might be a bit harsh. I'm sure there were no ill intentions; however, the yelling, whining, fake burping, and throwing of French fries made my five-year-old turn to me and say, "Whoa."

The saddest part was the sweet tone of the mommy saying, "Ok sweetie. Let's be good. Sit down. Here honey, eat the French fry. Mommy will get you more soda if you stay in your seat. OK, just stand up if you want instead." All I could think was "Oh, my God. I'd hate to meet up with this bunch when they are fourteen or fifteen years old." Judgmental on my part, perhaps, but that was my honest thought.

My response back to my five-year old was, "Honey, nobody told those two kids that this is a restaurant." To which her response was, "Oh. Well, somebody should."

Burger King is not the finest restaurant you'll ever enter, but hey, it's a restaurant where meals are shared in a public setting, and manners should prevail. A simple bottom line here is, nothing says "*Brat*" like a kid with no manners.

Although some customs in our society have changed over the past decades, the use of manners is one that should still be intact. It truly is the parents' responsibility to teach, re-teach, stress, re-teach, point out and reinforce, and re-teach manners again and again if need be. Children are not born saying "please" and "thank you," nor do they automatically say "excuse me" when they burp. They are not born holding the door for an older person or respectfully responding with "You're welcome" when they are thanked by a person they may or may not know. They are not born saying "Thank you for inviting me" when they play at a friend's house. They are not born saying "Excuse me" when they have something to say, or better yet, waiting until the other person has finished uttering his or her thoughts. A child who learns these social expectations learns to appreciate and respect the people they encounter. More importantly, they gain acceptance into the social realms in which they live.

There is another important and vital lesson embedded in the ritual of "manners." Manners can be either verbalized or seen through various gestures. Silent manners include appropriate body language, providing personal space, shaking hands, and making eye contact. These exchanges, whether verbal or silent, place boundaries on the social interactions that our children become involved in every day. Somewhere along the line in our development, we learned the social graces that helped us distinguish right from wrong. This is always important information when interacting with other individuals.

A child, who has not been taught the manners society expects, stands out. He is quickly labeled "rude," "obnoxious," "or bratty." In fact, it may be that somebody (his parents) has not taught him the importance of manners as an integral part of our accepted social norms. The reality is that people like to be with people who use the social conventions they can expect. These social conventions place boundaries around our social interactions. Manners make our relationships more predictable and comfortable. We, as a part of a civilized society, typically like (and need) manners to define our social norms.

Guiding question 3 might be: "In ten years, will my child follow the social manners and norms that will allow her to be socially accepted by her peers?"

STEP 4—NO SUCH THING AS BEDTIME

Ever been at a grocery store at 10:00 p.m. and hear a mother or father yelling at their child for throwing a "hissy fit" in the middle of the aisle because the child wants the cereal that comes with the special spoon? Ever been to an amusement park after dark only to witness a mom and dad snapping at each other as one of them is carrying the screaming kid under their right arm? Ever stare at a kid at the beach, on a warm summer day, as he grabs every toy he sees and think "What a brat." only to have the mom lean over to you and say, "He is tired. We took him to a baseball game last night and he didn't go to bed until after midnight."? I can only ask, "What? Are you all, nuts? These kids need sleep. I am pretty bratty too when I am tired."

Think about it.

Feeling cranky? Go to bed. Feeling overwhelmed? Maybe we need a nap. Feeling tired trying to fit everything into a day, and it just doesn't fit? Go to sleep and dream of far-away places. Somewhere along the line, we've learned how to relax and let our body heal from a tough day. Our children need to learn that, too.

During sleep, our bodies work overtime to grow and heal. Young children are growing constantly and the research shows that a good portion of their twenty-four-hour day needs to be devoted to sleep. This physical development needs time to happen during uninterrupted, restful sleep.

We live in a face-paced society where the adults and children are over-stimu-lated, over-programmed, and often over-tired. For their own long-term physical, emotional, and mental health, it is our obligation to help our children learn how to unwind and rest. We must teach them controlled relaxation. We need to reduce the stress and excitement right before bedtime so our children can learn to appreciate the quiet stillness and allow their bodies to ease into a restful sleep. The development of good sleep habits is important for a lifetime of good sleep patterns. Bedtime rituals and routines help to establish the predictable nature of unwinding before bedtime. Many families get in pajamas, brush their teeth, read before bed, say a prayer, kiss good night, and then turn off the lights. Other fam-ilies have a variety of rituals including a set of activities to set the stage for bed-time. Perhaps they include arranging the stuffed animals, talking about their day, planning out the events of tomorrow, or reading from the Bible. Whatever the ritual is, if done on a regular basis, it becomes second nature, and the routine itself helps the child learn to relax from a busy day and get the necessary rest that is critical to his development.

Another added bonus connected to established bedtime routines is personal expectations. Children who have a routine realize they are expected to set their own limits. If the routine is that they watch a particular show, turn off the TV, brush their teeth, kiss Mom and Dad good night, then get into bed, and if this routine is followed on a regular basis, the child will learn to monitor his own rou-tine and set his own limits. One day, to your own shock and delight, that child will follow the routine without prompting. He will get up, turn off the TV, kiss you good night, and put himself to bed, without you saying a word. For my chil-dren, it happened by four years of age. To my friends' amusement, the routine for all four children occurred at 6:30 p.m. until my oldest was in fifth grade. They had learned to set their own limits and came to expect the routine. My standard line back to my friends who got a kick out of this was, "There's no bonding after 7 p.m." Thus, 6:30 p.m. was a perfect bedtime for a long time.

For me, as a working mom, this routine had a beneficial side effect. It allowed a time for my husband and me to "regroup." We had some time for ourselves to focus on our relationship, once the kids went to bed. Often many moms will tell me that they can't get time with their spouse because the kids are always up until 9 or 10 p.m. Parents need to establish boundaries around their children's bed-time, so they can nurture their own relationship. Parents, whether single or in partnership, need to have the energy and commitment to raise healthy, well-rested, children.

Guiding question 4 might be: "In ten years, will my child be able to unwind from a busy day, clear his mind, and put himself into a deep state of relaxation so that he can remain healthy and strong?"

STEP 5—REPEAT YOURSELF OVER AND OVER

Brats don't happen overnight. It takes time—time for them to learn that the parent will repeat herself again and again, if need be. A child reasons, "Why do something the first time if I know I'm going to have several invitations to do the task?" Why would she want to clean her room, rake the yard, pick up her backpack, put her shoes away, or do anything else for that matter when she is busy watching TV or working on her own agenda?

The easy way out to reduce our own frustration would be to stop expecting them to listen the first time. After all, they've never had to do it so far. We can continue to repeat ourselves. Eventually, maybe, our baby will listen. Or will he?

What would happen if a parent said, "Come now or I am leaving," and the mother did? "Pick up your stuff or I am throwing it all out," and it actually happened? "Pick up your shoes or else I'll hide them," and then the shoes were hidden for a day or two?

This may seem severe, but the child will get the message that his parents mean what they said the first time. No, a child will not listen every time a parent opens her mouth, but idle threats are just that—idle. After a while, no one listens or responds to them. By teaching our children that we mean what we say, respect and trust are developed. These two concepts are the foundations for every relationship our children will have—with us, siblings, peers, friends, their future partner, and everyone they will ever come in contact with.

Respect doesn't just happen. It is learned and earned. It is fragile and can be misrepresented. It can be self-centered or other-centered. Respect is a continuum that goes between the self and others. Brats have a high regard and respect for themselves, and a low respect for others. This is a behavior and mindset that is learned. If respect is taught, then likewise, lack of respect is also taught. What we value and teach our children is critical. Teaching them to respect appropriate requests the first time around will ultimately teach them to show respect for others.

Trust is a timeless necessity. Like respect, it too is fragile beyond words. It can take years to develop trust in relationships and moments to tear it down. Trust between parents and children begin with follow-through between words and actions. If there's a match between the two, a child will learn to trust what is said. But, when there is a mismatch, there will ultimately be mistrust and doubt. Children learn to predict and expect certain actions and/or reactions based on repeated experiences. When trust is developing, there must be a critical match between words and actions.

Nothing drives me crazier than hearing a parent say five times, "This is the last time I'm going to say this." All I think of is the famous cartoon of the dog thinking, "Blah, blah, blah, cookie, blah, blah, blah, blah." The fact is, if we say, "This is the last time I'm saying this," then we have to make sure it *is* the last time. Otherwise, our children will not learn to trust our words. Therefore, the lack of respect is being rewarded through more opportunities to do what is asked of him.

The bottom line is if we say it, we have to mean it, or else we're sending mixed messages. If we don't mean it, then we don't say it. We should pick something else to say—something that matches our actions to our words, or aligns our words to the actions we intend to take.

Guiding question 5 might be: "In ten years will my child value, trust, and respect my words as we grow older together?"

Step 6—Make Excuses for Them

Back when we were kids, what happened when we forgot our lunch money at home? Did the world end when we forgot to bring our violin in for our lesson? Did everything fall apart when we didn't do our chores? Of course life went on. We actually learned some important problem-solving and self-advocacy skills. We had to rely on ourselves to seek alternative options and/or face the consequences. We lived through it and learned from it.

Then why is it that we often feel compelled to "fix everything" for our children? Isn't there a life lesson in forgetting something once, whether it is your lunch money, violin, or emptying the dishwasher? There are natural consequences that sometimes are extremely valuable lessons. All children need to learn that their actions or lack of actions have natural consequences. These natural consequences are a fact of life and sometimes occur without the child having the ability to control the severity of the consequences.

Forgetting lunch money is a great example. For the day, the child might have to rely on his self-advocacy skills and ask the cafeteria manager to charge his lunch or solicit a friend to loan him money. These consequences are not life altering, but this lesson from this one day may serve as a life-long lesson that will stay with him far longer than just ten years.

Another example might involve procrastination. At 9:00 p.m., when the child has had two weeks to complete a project, it's a given that the computer will freeze or the printer will run out of ink. When we look to the "guideline sheet" the teacher had provided, it clearly states "Plan ahead. No excuses." This would probably be a perfect time for a discussion about the consequences of procrastination. We then need to allow our child the opportunity to accept and deal with these consequences. This is the tricky, somewhat uncomfortable, part for many parents. But it is the necessary part for the children to learn from.

When a child is in a predicament and Mom and Dad are not there to "excuse" his way out of it, the child must rely on his own problem-solving skills and take responsibility for himself. Few people would dispute the argument that problem solving and self-advocacy skills are crucial to being successful in our society. Through repeated opportunities, throughout childhood, to experience these skills, a child can learn to use them, fine tune them, and analyze the results of them. Their successes reinforce their skills, and their failures allow them to reassess their problem-solving strategies, alter them, and try again. When we step in to save the day and excuse the child, all in the name of saving them from painful experiences—natural or imposed—we interfere with this critical learning cycle.

These natural consequences teach our children to take responsibility for themselves. When we make excuses for our children, we rob them of these lessons. Sometimes the direct correlation between the child's action (or inaction as the case may be) and the natural consequences that will occur is far more powerful than anything we can create for the child.

Realistically, there are times when the excuses we make for our children are grounded in facts. For example, a child who has attention deficit disorder (ADD) with or without hyperactivity and frequently forgets things or acts impulsively has issues he must learn to deal with. Strategies must be taught and made available so that the likelihood of success is within reach. However, the consequences that are attached to the reality of the situation are still valuable lessons for the child. If we constantly make excuses for the child, when will we know if the child can incorporate some simple strategies to mange his own life?

Here's an example. I have recently come across a mom who seems to want to make her son out to be more handicapped than he actually is. The boy has ADD and is on medication to help the situation. Every time he "forgets" something, however, Mom does not want him held to the same accountability level as his peers. Her reasoning is one big excuse—the ADD won't allow him be normal. I find this from my perspective frustrating and crippling from the boy's perspective. I believe that the natural consequences of forgetting an assignment—a homework slip, teacher reminder, even a school detention—may allow him to experience a consequence that could help him in the future. The boy is so shielded by Mom's constant reminders and excuses that it is hard to find the opportunities to praise his successful moments.

I might add that this boy walks around in one of two modes: either looking as if he is afraid of his own shadow or acting cocky and responding with "I forgot. I'll have my mom call you." He has learned that he does not have to be accountable, as he has a built-in excuse. By holding him accountable for his actions (or lack of actions) he may, in fact, learn that to avoid unwanted consequences, he must rely on strategies to compensate for his attention deficit disorder. I believe children are very capable of learning how to manage their affairs successfully, even in the face of difficulties, whether they are academic, physical, or emotional, when they are given the opportunities to deal with consequences and make connections between their actions and consequences. This takes time and patience on the parents' part.

Guiding question 6 might be: "In ten years, will my child be able to hold himself accountable for his own behaviors, and handle things as they arise?"

STEP 7—WHAT'S A COMMITMENT?

Long ago, way back in the 1970s, my sister couldn't go to the movies to see *Tommy* (Now, there's an old movie some of you have never even heard of.) because she had a babysitting job lined up for the night. The "brat" in her reared its ugly head as she and my mother battled it out. My sister wanted to feign illness, break her leg, or take on a mysterious disease—anything to get out of babysitting. That's when I first heard the word "commitment." I thought Mom was just being a ball-buster, but she was serious, and my sister did not go see the movie that night. She had to baby-sit.

I think of this childhood scenario whenever a mother calls the school to help her baby "find the loophole," "create an excuse," or straight out lie for her child, and thus break a commitment. How sad. What a lost opportunity to learn a lifelong lesson about commitment.

I don't want to seem too cynical. There are some real events that force us all to change our plans, but a play-date versus a teacher appointment is not one of them. An impromptu baseball practice versus a school detention is not one of them. A last-minute invitation to a "popular" girl's party versus a committed response to go to someone else's party is certainly not one of them. These all fall under the category of "breaking a commitment."

A "brat" doesn't care about this commitment thing because he's learned that his needs, interests, and desires take precedence over other people's needs, interests, and desires. He's been raised to believe that his feelings are what matter first.

In my opinion, we are all a little bit responsible for helping each other get through life. This is actually a big and powerful responsibility. The reality is that all children need to learn that their actions affect others in ways that may not be obvious at first. Following through on a commitment shows someone else that they are important. Honoring a commitment affects others in a positive way. Breaking a commitment, unnecessarily, has an opposite effect on people. This action tells people they are less important and not a priority.

As humans, we all have a need to believe we can control our lives and situations as they arise. This control gives us a sense of security in some ways. By adolescence, it is critical that control begins to shift from parent to adolescent. They need practice managing their lives, situations, and commitments. As parents, we have an obligation to teach our children that they have this locus of control over their commitments, the ability to manage their commitments, and the obligation to keep their commitments. Our children will be judged by their peers throughout their lives on how well their actions match their words. Their ability to follow through on commitments will affect them personally and professionally throughout their lives. And so we are faced with another guiding question:

Guiding question 7 might be: "In ten years, will my child be perceived by the world as one who can make a commitment and stay true to it?"

STEP 8—COMPUTERS UNLIMITED

Talking to the black box—that's what I call Instant Messaging (IM-ing for the really cool folks out there). This sounds dramatic, but it scares me to death. Back in my day (I always hated that line), we were introduced to the "total phone." We'd call one person without them knowing a second person was on the line. We'd trap them into saying something about person number two and then nail them. Yes, it was mean. (Meanness has been around a long time.) Yes, it was embarrassing when you were person number three saying something mean or negative about person number two even though person number one made you feel safe during a "confidential" conversation. The question has to be asked, "Who is the bigger culprit? Number one for tricking number three, or number three for saying something mean about number two?"

The debate could go on forever, but the fact remains that there will be some fall-out over this type of situation. Some people would call this a natural consequence for inappropriate behavior. (Refer back to Step 6.) And yes, it was likely that we were held accountable for our words by our peers the next day at school. The "next day" always seems to come.

Today, instant messaging adds a whole new level of scariness to growing up. It is a modern-day variation of yesterday's total phone call. Screen names are used (and not always by their rightful owners), anonymity is kept, and emotions stay out of it while fingers type away. Furthermore, the ability to deny the cruel instant messages typed "anonymously" is a real temptation for our children. Denial is an easy way to escape the consequences of their poorly judged, or hastily typed, conversations. I've dealt with this nonsense at school, and have become more adamant about my feelings toward it.

Instant messaging does not encourage emotional development. It does not enhance a child's social skills. Quite frankly, kids don't need it. They may want it, but they don't need it (Quick—go back and reread Step 2). Now, I know that many people believe instant messaging goes hand in hand with modern technology, and they believe it is necessary for educational reasons. I do not deny that there are many benefits to computers, but I cannot bring myself to fully believe that the pros outweigh the cons of instant messaging, unless a child is engaged in a conversation with a real-live scientist through the use of instant messaging. And, if this is the case, please be sure it really is a real-live scientist, which is a whole other level of necessary vigilance!

I am in no way advocating the destruction of all computers. What I am advocating is strong parental supervision, limited access to instant messaging, and open dialogue with our children about the damaging effect that "meanness" via the computer can have on another child. And, when they are on the receiving end of the meanness, we need to be ready to discuss it with our children. It is almost sure to happen sooner or later.

We need to be extremely cautious with instant messaging if we choose to allow it in our homes. It can be devastating because children can type very mean things into a black box and feel anonymous. Emotionally, they may not be mature enough to handle it. If a parent can't monitor it appropriately, remember, the child can live without it. Millions of children around the world survive without instant messaging. If they want to "talk" to a friend, they can use the phone. Better yet, they can invite some friends over to talk, "hang out," and eat pizza. Parents will get to know who their child's friends are this way, far better than if the child simply talks to their friends through instant messaging.

Beyond instant messaging is the great World Wide Web. Valuable uses are abundant, and it allows children and adults to access the world, other individuals, literature, sciences, cultures around the world and so much more. It is a powerful and truly amazing, mind-blowing invention. With all that being said, the flip side is that there are very real dangers directly associated with unsupervised Internet use. Chat rooms, websites and e-mails are everywhere in the media. Pedophiles pose as nice guys, older men pose as potential "boyfriends," young girls hide their true identities and instantly become interesting women. Before you know it, they're in too deep, and, in the worse scenarios, they are dead. (Feel free to read the book *Katie.com*. It's a wake-up call to every parent.)

I know I sound a bit paranoid, and I am. Just think about this. We would never leave a gun in our adolescent's bedroom, and we teach our babies from the time they are old enough to speak to not talk to strangers. Yet many (way too many) parents allow their children to have a screen name at the early ages of eight or nine, to have a bio put onto AOL, or to have a computer in their rooms as a pre-teen. My fear is that I believe every twelve-year-old is tempted by the Internet in the wee hours of the night. Some parents encourage their children to create their own website with personal information on it because it *so* creative and innovative. This could be a deadly disaster for your child. Sorry to sound so dramatic, but I have seen the printouts from the chat rooms children "talk" in. I have seen some screen names for twelve-year-old girls and boys that make me blush. I bet parents would be shocked—I know I was the first time. And they often, very often, are not the kids you'd expect to have screen names like these. These are the "good kids." These are kids, just like yours and mine.

The Internet brings the world into our homes. As an educator, I value what a wonderful opportunity for learning this presents. As a parent, I recognize that it is an unbelievable risk and responsibility. Our children's exposure to everything in the world is at his fingertips. Yes, we can monitor it. Yes, we can set all the parental controls. Yes, we can limit our children's time and sit with them while they search the net. We should do all these things and more. We should take an active role in learning all we can about the computer gadgets and the Internet so that we are on the same playing field as our children when it comes to dealing with technology.

One final note on limiting computer time. By doing so, we reinforce the need to set boundaries. (Quick, reread Step 2.) Limits and boundaries make kids feel safe. Boundaries are a good thing. When the lines are nonexistent or blurred, the safe feelings kids need (even if they won't admit it) are diminished, and they may end up in a potentially dangerous position and/or one that is uncomfortable at a gut level. Furthermore, learning to set limits and boundaries when your children are young can help them set their own limits when they are out on their own in the big scary world. This is a healthy, life-long skill. Computers can be a fabulous tool for communication and seeking information, but our children must be kept safe. They must learn to use the technology available to them responsibly. Their security is our responsibility. This is a parent's job.

Guiding question 8 might be: "In ten years, will my child be able to set limits that keep her safe in the ever-widening world in which she'll live?"

STEP 9—TRULY BELIEVE THEY ARE THE CENTER OF THE WORLD

Of course, it is okay to tell our children they are the center of Mom's world or the apple of Daddy's eye. And often, although our lives do revolve around our children, that doesn't mean they are special to everyone else around them. I know this sounds harsh, but think of it this way for a minute. The neighbor's kid is a bit of a nudge, has a loud annoying laugh, and big ears. Our children, on the other hand, are sweet, compassionate, and attractive. The neighbor kid's parents' world revolves around their child, just as ours does around our children. There is no difference between the love and special bond they have for their kid, and the love and special bond we have for ours. So each time we think that surely everyone appreciates our "special center of the world," we are kidding ourselves. Although our children are special to us, they are just not that special to everyone else around them.

Here's a reality check to consider. If we continue to believe our children are the center of the world and the sun rises and shines upon them, we will hear ourselves say things like this: "I am not sure that you are aware of how 'sensitive' my child is to everyone." (We have to remember that we are not with our children around the clock, in school, or at the park when no other adults are there.) "Surely it wasn't my child who gave his work to the other kid (someone else's special center of the world). The other kid must have stolen it and copied it." "I know there are standards, and I am not asking you to lower the standard or cut-off criteria, but if you could just make an exception for him, I am sure you'll see how great he really is in math." (If he was that great, perhaps he would have made the cut-off criteria.) When we hear ourselves uttering a phrase similar to any of these, we need to take a deep breath and pause to reflect a bit. It's important to be honest with ourselves about how we might be viewing our children. Do we place our children at the center of the world, or simply as part of the world?

Egocentricity is an important part of growing up. It allows us to focus on ourselves and compare ourselves to the world. And, of course, there are normal egocentric developmental milestones that all children must go through. It is always our hope that our children will pass these milestones; however, we as parents must move past these egocentric phases before our children can. We can expect our children to believe they are the center of all humanity and the universe at certain points of development, but not forever. We must always keep an adult perspective on this and not fall into the trap of believing their egocentric views. They will grow out of it, mature and begin to see their role in the universe, but we must always be vigilant of their development and help them keep it in perspective.

As they grow and develop and move through their egocentric phases, it is important for a child to realize that he is not the center of everybody's world. Equally important is the fact that they need something to be at the center of their being. This brings me to a topic some people don't want to think about, but there is a need to bring it up. I am not a "holy roller" nor do I preach my beliefs wherever I go. (I may lose some of you here, but that's okay—just skip this part if you don't want to read it.)

I have a strong belief in God, the Universal One, angels, and the work of the Holy Spirit. I fully believe there is a power far stronger than any one of us individually—one that holds us all together. This is the same powerful force I believed knew my every move as a kid and helped to keep me "within bounds" when my parents weren't around. I believe our children must have faith or a belief system that is bigger than they are and bigger than Mom and Dad. Some things can't be fixed by Mom and Dad and sometimes our children have to believe there is something or someone that will help them get through the tough times of growing up. Faith, religion, a spiritual grounding—whatever you want to call it—is important, perhaps vital, to a child's well being. Children will be faced with hundreds of challenging choices to make. They need a grounding force or belief system to turn to—a rudder to keep them on an even keel. Faith, or a belief in something much bigger than themselves, will give them this grounding. How you instill this belief system into their lives is your family's choice. My only message here is give them something to believe in that will help guide them as they learn to make decisions throughout their lives.

A "subquestion" we may want to ask ourselves, which is connected to this issue of faith, may be, "In ten years, will my child have a faith base to lean on when times get tough?" Whether we see faith as a separate entity or an interwoven thread to the core of our children's developmental path is ultimately a choice each one of us has to make. But faith can help our children see beyond themselves to a greater purpose.

Egocentricity is important for emotional development, but a child can't stay there forever if she is to become an emotionally healthy adult. We, the parents, must help our children see that they are not the center of the world. In fact, something far bigger than themselves may be part of a greater and very necessary belief system. This belief system is established and nurtured by us as parents. Later in life, our children will need a foundation on which to build their own faith journey. The groundwork we lay now will be the focal point of their faith journey, which will lead them from an egocentric view of the world to finding and fulfilling their purpose in this world. From a parent's perspective, it is an awesome experience to watch this belief system emerge and become strong.

Guiding question 9 might be: "In ten years, will my child be able to see the world from another person's perspective and realize her own influence and purpose in the world?"

STEP 10—ACT AS IF THEY ARE IN CONTROL

Children are born trying to learn to control their environment. At a very early age they learn that crying gets them food, and crying gets them the physical contact they need in order to thrive, and crying also gets them "live entertainment" from Mom, Dad, or Grandma.

By the time the child is two, he has learned that many circumstances in his environment can be manipulated by his actions. Tantrums develop as identity and separation issues arise. Sometimes an out-of-control temper tantrum gets parents jumping up and asking such things as, "Do you want water?" (Is the kid breaking into a sweat?) "Do you want to go to bed?" (What kid will ever answer, "Bingo, Mom, that's it."?) "Do you want to stop now?" (Why should he? He's got your full attention now.) The bottom line is these children are learning acceptable ways to handle frustration and control their environment. All kids need boundaries to feel safe, secure, and accepted, whether they are two hours old, two years old, twelve years old, or twenty-two years old. Familiarity with these boundaries begins early on and will set the stage for future challenging opportunities in their lives.

As the parents, we must set limits. At the risk of sounding like a broken record, the development of self-control and setting limits and boundaries are critical in today's world for our children. This fact can not be stated too much. There is no easy way around this. If we act as though our children are in control, the boundaries will not be set, and the foundation for future learning will not be solid. I am not saying that we need to be dictators and not allow the child's input; I am saying that the boundaries must be evident and managed on a regular basis.

The stakes are too high for children who have never had the boundaries drawn, reinforced and respected. It seems impossible that what a parent does with her two-year old has any direct link to their future twelve-year old; however, it does. Far too often, parents will sit in my office as I am dealing with their child on a discipline issue and say, "You know. I never could control his temper tantrums. How do you expect me to control him now when he is with his friends?"

The reality is that we really cannot control our children's friends, or even our own children, for that matter. The truth is we can really only control ourselves. Therefore, if we haven't ever laid the groundwork for self-control with boundaries when the kid was two, it will seem nearly impossible to start laying it when he is twelve. An absence of limits in the world of a twelve-year old has much greater risks connected to it than in the world of a two-year old: drinking, friends, parties, drugs, and sexual activity (See Part IV: The Big Scary World).

I will share an example of an experience of a two-year old. Stephanie was two and a half years old when we went to my parents' house in New York. Sharon, my friend, had come with me. She had no children of her own and we both taught at the middle school level together. Many of our private conversations had revolved around boundaries (or lack of) regarding our students.

While visiting, Stephanie threw down an empty cup because she had finished the contents and wanted to go play. My response was "Pick up the cup."

Hers was, "No."

I finally got comfortable on the floor, since I realized we were not going to agree very quickly. I had trapped her with my body in a portion of the kitchen and each time Stephanie tried to walk away, I'd push the cup to her and say "Pick up the cup." After forty-five minutes of Stephanie's tears and refusals to comply, Stephanie finally did pick up the cup, gave me a smirk and ran off to go play.

Sharon and I laughed out loud knowing that a critical "line in the sand" had been drawn.

I don't know whether it was my professional experience, my gut feeling as a mom, my Irish stubbornness, or because my friend was watching me carefully, that made me stick to this issue for so long, but I realize now what a critical moment that was for Stephanie and me to establish a boundary between us. She learned that I was going to establish the guidelines, stick to them, and insist she follow them. She also learned that her mom could be a stubborn pain in the…who loved her enough to set a boundary and standard for her. She was not in control of the situation and yet she began to learn self-control in the end. As a fourteen-year old now, Stephanie and I have shared many of these "control" moments. We understand who is in control during these hard times and where the line of control can and will be drawn. My firm belief is when our kids are out of control we need to stay in control. We need to help them see that the world still has boundaries, they need to monitor their self-control, and their safety always comes first.

Guiding question 10 might be: "In ten years, will my child be able to set boundaries for herself that are aligned with my expectations for keeping her safe?"

STEP 11—LET THEM YELL "I HATE YOU" WHENEVER THEY FEEL LIKE IT

Nothing drives me crazier than hearing a two-year old yell, "I hate you," until I hear an eight-year old say it, then a twelve-year old. We can try to justify it by saying, "I am teaching my child to express himself and let go of his anger." We may believe that, or we may be so embarrassed that we don't know what else to say.

In my years as a parent (fifteen, so far) and as a teacher and administrator (eighteen, so far), I have never had a child say that to me out loud. However, I have been in the presence of children when they say it to their mother (usually), and regardless of the circumstances, I always find it disturbing. I cannot think of a single situation when this type of behavior and language would be acceptable.

A major responsibility of parenting is teaching respect. Respect can be given, encouraged, demonstrated, and shared, but it can never be demanded or controlled. Respect comes from experiences that have been reinforced over time. Respect is learned by children, through the modeled actions of the adults around them. We, as parents, are the primary educators. Our children will learn the most from our interactions with the world around us and with how we respectfully treat them. If we treat people around us with respect, even if we are angry or don't particularly care for them as individuals, we can still model respect when we are in the presence of our children. We will have to dig deep into our assertive, non-aggressive responses and make decisions about dealing with this person, but for the long-term benefit for our children, we must handle the whole situation with respect. We need to be aware of our reactions to others. How often do our children hear, "I hate so and so"? We are the ultimate role model for respect. We must be cautious with our words so that our children learn to be cautious with their words.

Respect builds as opportunities arise to discuss what it is. It is not a tangible object that a parent can "show" her child, but it is something that a parent can demonstrate every day in every situation. There are times it is difficult, but it is always necessary to put it out there as an expectation and part of a parent's typical mode of operation. In time, the child will be faced with difficulties with peers, a teacher, a spouse, or employer. They need to be able to handle the situation in a manner that is productive for them. Respect is key during these difficult times. Respect allows an individual to remain confident and clear in many situations. I'd be hard pressed to find a parent who wouldn't agree that respect has been an important component in his or her own successful personal and professional relationships.

Guiding question 11 might be: "In ten years, will my child respect and value the individuals with whom he interacts on a daily basis?"

And so, here are 11 easy steps, which, if carefully followed, will produce a brat. I'm sure there are many other additional steps that can be taken to supplement these steps to ensure a healthy brat. I say this with complete sarcasm and respect for the awesome job of raising healthy children who can cope with life as adults. My humor is an attempt to highlight key "running themes" that are vital to the development of all children. The themes, embedded in the previous pages, include:

• Fostering delayed gratification and patience

• Setting boundaries that safely allow for choices while providing limits

- Developing social graces and social boundaries that allow social acceptance into peer groups

- Establishing routines and limits that allow children to learn to set personal limits and maintain self-control

- Enforcing rest, which is critical for a healthy body, mind, and spirit

- Remembering that our words have valuable meanings, and our actions must match our words

- Teaching that trust and respect are timeless necessities

- Allowing natural consequences, which provide valuable learning opportunities

- Modeling that we are accountable for our behaviors and actions

- Showing how commitments and follow-through define us to the world

- Encouraging a belief in something bigger than ourselves

- Instilling the idea that respect is earned and valuable

Parenting is not easy, but I believe it is the most important and most rewarding task ever achieved by any human. To accomplish this unbelievable task, we must always balance and think about the long-range goals of raising children versus the short-term day-to-day moments that can put us in a parenting conflict easily. It is always important to keep the critical nature of these running themes in our minds.

Again, I present the 11 Guiding Questions that we might ask ourselves when dealing with our children at every age. We should reread these often and answer them honestly every chance we get. What kind of kids do we want to have living in our house in ten years? The choice really is ours.

In ten years—

1. *Will my child be able to have the patience to work hard and delay his gratification so that he may receive what he truly needs, not just what he wants?*

2. *Will the "no" matter?*

3. *Will my child follow the social manners and norms that will allow her to be socially accepted by her peers?*

4. *Will my child be able to unwind from a busy day, clear his mind, and put himself into a deep state of relaxation so that he can remain healthy and strong?*

5. *Will my child value, trust, and respect my words as we grow older together?*

6. *Will my child be able to hold himself accountable for his own behaviors and handle things as they arise?*

7. *Will my child be perceived by the world as one who can make a commitment and stay true to it?*

8. *Will my child be able to set limits that keep her safe in the ever-widening world in which she'll live?*

9. *Will my child be able to see the world from another person's perspective and realize her own influence and purpose in the world?*

10. *Will my child be able to set boundaries for herself that are aligned with my expectations for keeping her safe?*

11. *Will my child respect and value the individuals with whom he interacts on a daily basis?*

Part II:

The Great Adventure: The Teacher-Parent Conference

Up until the time a child goes to kindergarten his parent may have been with him much of the time. If he went to preschool or a day care provider Mom was probably given daily sheets about every detail of his day. Regardless of the path the child had been on, until this point in time, his parents knew what he had for breakfast, what time was naptime, how long he slept for, who he played with, and every gory detail about his bowel movements.

And then kindergarten happens.

For my children, kindergarten was a four-hour cut in their day. They had been going to day care from 7:00 a.m. to almost 5:00 p.m. since they were very little. When public school came into their world, their school day was dropped from 9:00 a.m. to 3:00 p.m. However, with the decrease in hours for them, also came a decrease in "knowing the details of their day" for me. As a working mom, it was not possible for me to be a volunteer in their classes on a regular basis. My vacation time was really the only time I could be the volunteer classroom mom.

When other moms talked about being in their child's classroom, or worse yet, my kid's classroom, each week or for all the special days, it made me cringe. It still does sometimes. Being a public school educator, I couldn't take time off during a school day for all the special activities. I was expected to be in my students' classrooms, not my children's classrooms. I had to make a conscious decision to not buy into the guilt of not being available to volunteer in their classrooms.

I realized quickly that if I allowed them to, people could make me feel guilty, intentionally or perhaps unintentionally, in very subtle and not-so-subtle ways. For example, below are some statements to watch out for. All are real quotes that have been said directly to me. Some seemed intentionally evil to me, although they were probably not intended to be evil. It's all in the ear of the receiver. All of the comments either ticked me off or made me cry back then. Time does heal some of them, but some of the scars on my heart are deep.

- "They can't get any drivers to go on the fieldtrips. They'll have to cancel it if we don't get more moms. It's a shame you have to work and won't be able to drive." (My response now is "Big deal. Millions of kids will never go to the Bronx Zoo and I am sure they will survive." Back then I walked away and said nothing aloud.)

- "I have to set up for the Valentine's party because none of the moms in Vincent's (my kid) class will come in." (My response now is "Those parties are always at the same busy time in every public school. It's just the nature of the timing." Back then I just walked away and said nothing out loud.)

- "The principal asked me to take on this committee because I am the one who is always here at the school." (My thinking now is "Aren't you a hero, or a martyr, who can't or won't say no.")

- "Oh, what do you know. You made it to Kevin's (my son) concert." (What I did say was, "Yes, I was able to scoot out a little bit early today." What I wanted to say was, "Don't you think it kills me inside to miss all the other events, you wench.")

- And my personal favorite: "Why don't you like coming to the end-of-the-year PTO party where we honor all the moms who give so much of their time to always be here for all the children?" (*Yuck.* One end-of-the-year party for me and I left crying; swearing I'd never attend another. I don't know if it was envy, jealousy, guilt, or a feeling of being left out of my child's day-to-day school life that was the overriding feeling. I will probably never be 100 percent sure.)

So how can we be a part of our child's day and get as much information about the details as possible when we work full time and have a professional and personal life to juggle? The key is to open up as many communication channels as possible. We can go to PTO meetings even though they are at night and we are exhausted. We can talk to a few close friends who are those active moms we secretly envy, but know that their work benefits our children as well. And, most importantly, never miss a parent conference.

Parent-teacher conferences are invaluable moments that allow us to open the doors of communication and see into our child's day. Most schools schedule them well in advance, and generally parents can request them whenever they feel the need by directly contacting their child's teacher. Take advantage of this opportunity. It helps to level the playing field for all working parents. I call the parent-teacher conference "The Great Adventure" because that's what it is. Two people who know the same child come together with two different perspectives about that child. There must be some risk-taking, communication, trust, and good listening skills practiced during the conference to make this adventure together a great one.

Our baby is an emotional issue for us, but for a parent-teacher conference we have to use our head to share and gather as much information as possible. The following questions can help parents get the "biggest bang for their buck" with regard to working with the teacher and getting a clear understanding of what their child's day is like. Two key factors throughout any conference are to *keep an open mind* and *listen with your head and your heart.*

"What are my personal feelings about school?"

We bring our own feelings and past experiences into everything we do. Going into a parent-teacher conference is no exception. We should pay attention to our own feelings about school. When we enter our child's school, we need to pay attention to our "gut feelings." We should ask ourselves questions such as Did *I* like second grade? Did *I* like my fourth-grade teacher? Was *I* a "good" student? Did *my* fifth-grade teacher yell a lot? Think about this. Give some reflective thought to your own perceptions and feelings about school. There may be deep emotions we've been harboring that we may need to deal with so we can put them to the side and deal effectively with our child's teacher about our child. If we become anxious, based on our own view of "the teacher," we may not ask the right questions. Don't let your own emotions and memories block you from learning about your child's school experience.

We may project anger or fear toward this person who simply represents or reminds us of a past experience. This person may remind us of a teacher we once knew, and subconsciously we may project our own feelings onto the teacher based on our personal past experiences. A key point is to be aware of our thoughts, words, and behaviors. When we say to our child's teacher at the confer-ence, "I remember my second-grade teacher used to..." or "You look just like my fifth-grade teacher" or "I always hated school, and I am sure Johnny feels the same way.", we must be aware of the experiences we have had that we are filtering the conference through.

A word of caution about these possible projections and verbalizations because we've all "done school," but our experiences vary greatly. We need to be aware of our own experiences, attitudes, and projections on what we perceive to be school. The more we are aware of our own emotional history associated with school, teachers, and learning, the more available we will be to an open dialogue about our children's school experiences.

Prior to going into the conference, it may be helpful to openly discuss our feelings about our past experiences with someone we trust. This strategy may help us to stay more focused on our children's educational needs and experiences without being distracted by the self-talk in our heads. Our personal feelings and experiences about school are important, but the focus of the conference must be on our children.

"When do I ask for a conference?"

In general, most public elementary schools schedule conferences for every student at various points throughout the year. Many of these schools schedule a fall conference and a spring conference. By the time a child reaches middle school, the general conferences usually end. Many parents might believe that is the end of getting information about their child, but that is a complete myth. Generally speaking, parents can request a conference regarding their child's academic performance at any time. The shape and participants in the conference may, however, vary between school and grade levels. For example, perhaps a representative teacher and guidance counselor may be able to meet with the parent or the parent may have the opportunity to meet with all of the child's teachers simultaneously at a team meeting, if teaming is a part of the school culture. Regardless of who may be involved, a parent's question frequently is "When should I ask for a conference?"

The short answer is "anytime a parent has a concern." The reality is the answer is a bit more complex. To me, the real answer falls into two categories: reactive reasons and proactive reasons. Reactive reasons to request a conference might be failing grades, a change in the child's excitement about school, recent conflicts with peers, an increase in behavioral problems either at home or at school, or a host of other reasons that are beyond typical developmental behaviors that cause parents to wonder, "What's going on with him?"

If the school has not taken the initiative to call a parent in to talk about her child, then the parent needs to take the initiative to have a focused conversation about her child and her concerns. Quite often parents think the school will know relevant information as part of their knowledge about all kids. However, the reality is that any given teacher deals with a multitude of issues and pieces of information about every kid all day. As the parent, it is often critical that we highlight our child's past history, educational issues that may resurface year after year, or "soft signs" that we know about our child that are relevant for the teachers to know. This is our parental responsibility. They have, perhaps, one hundred students to keep in mind. A parent has one important student of theirs. The parent knows her child best.

Proactive reasons differ from reactive reasons in that parents are seeking to avoid a problem, gain information, or share information in an attempt to avoid failing grades and increases in behavioral problems. Parents are seeking to proactively stimulate excitement about school with their child, or enhance their child's educational experience in some way. As a working parent, who is not available to be at the school frequently, a request for a conference allows me to show my child that she is important enough to take some time to personally meet all of her teachers. It allows me to focus all my thoughts on one of my children at a time and clarify his strengths and weaknesses on a regular basis. It also allows me to meet teachers and give them a personal invitation to call me at anytime, for good or bad reasons. I write my number out for them ahead of time and encourage them to call me at any moment. During this time, I believe teachers can get a quick synopsis of a child's needs without going through stacks of irrelevant papers looking for important bits of information about my specific kid. Most parents can sum up their kid's personality and educational needs in about seven sentences or less. Proactive conferences attempt to eliminate the need for reactive conferences. Truth be told, during a child's educational career, a parent will probably experience both.

Above all else, we must listen to our instincts. If we feel the need to see the teachers regarding our child, we should go ahead, be brave, and ask for a conference.

"What communication skills do I need?"

The communication skills that are needed during a conference are the same ones that we need to use whenever important information is being conveyed about a critical matter. In this case, our child is the critical matter, and his academic progress and classroom behavior is the important information that is being shared. Active listening skills need to be used. Paraphrasing and restating information is a useful technique. Focusing on what is being said and restating it back to the teacher, conveying just the facts and omitting any emotion may be difficult, but it will help us be sure we have a clear sense of our child's performance. For example:

- Teacher says: "Melissa has been helping people in class, but she often seems like she can't get her own work done in the limited time we have for math. I'm not sure if she knows the concepts yet, but I'm working on assessing her skills to determine her current performance level."

- Parent's response: "So what you are telling me is that she helps others, has a hard time getting her own work done, and you are in the process of getting a clearer picture of her math skills right now, correct?"

This type of paraphrasing allows the teacher to hear back the statements she said in order to check for clarity and accuracy. It also allows the parent to restate the teacher's comments to ensure that she takes home accurate information at the end of the conference. Asking clarifying questions can help to keep the conversation focused and meaningful. Open-ended and closed questions serve different purposes. Open-ended questions allow for a variety of responses. Closed questions limit the answers to one or two choices. Both are effective and important tools when the goal is to gain a deeper understanding of a child's classroom performance. Appropriate body language, paraphrasing and asking different types of questions are necessary communication skills that can serve to open up communication between a parent and the teacher. We need to remember that our goal is to gain all the information we can about our children from the person who spends up to seven hours with them each day. We should ask questions and communicate our concerns by using well-rehearsed communication skills.

"What questions should I ask?"

Using open-ended and closed questions, with skill, is an important technique in gaining information. Knowing which questions to ask at particular times is important and should be practiced in a variety of situations. Our child's conference provides us with a great forum to ask great questions focused on our child. However, many individuals replay a tape in their heads that sounds something like, "This may be a dumb question, but…" and it blocks their courage to ask their questions.

In reality, there *are* dumb questions. Nevertheless, at a parent-teacher conference a parent should never hesitate to ask a question that she needs answered about her child's development and education. If a parent honestly doesn't know the answer then the question should be asked, regardless if the questioner is afraid it will sound dumb. The goal is to ask meaningful and useful questions. Meaningful questions often start with the words "how" or "what." These questions are open-ended and seek more complex answers. Closed questions often have *yes* or *no* as their response. They are usually answered with one word and tend to shut down discussions. On the other hand, open-ended questions open up the conversation and press for specific information. These questions tend to carry and shape the conversation. During the conference, the parent will want to use both types of questions. Remember, though, the more open-ended questions, the more specific insights will likely be gained into a child's "school-time" world.

Here are some examples of good conferencing questions, but of course each parent-teacher conference will generate ones that are of importance to each parent and her child, at that point in time:

- How does _____ get along with his peers?

- Is _____ kind to other kids and respectful to adults? If so, what are some examples so that I can talk to _____ about how happy I am with his actions of kindness?

- In what areas do you have concerns for _____?

- What do you see as _____'s strong and/or weak areas?

- How does _____ handle classroom transitions?

- What are some strategies I can reinforce at home with _____ to increase _____'s ability to read, write, take turns, etc?

- Can you explain these test scores to me? How are these scores reflected in _____'s day to day activities?

There are a million questions that could and should be asked about our children. The order and focus of the questions will vary depending on the child's personality and his academic, social, and emotional needs. A parent's specific concerns and/or reasons for the conference will also dictate the direction and focus of the questions.

A conference can feel overwhelming. If a parent is afraid he will forget what he wants to ask, he should write down some questions before going to the conference. The questions should be prioritized since there probably will be a time limit on the conference, but a parent should feel absolutely comfortable bringing his written questions to the conference. If a parent thinks he'll need longer than the usual amount of scheduled time, he can ask the teacher, in advance, to schedule the conference for a longer time, or he can send the questions to the teacher ahead of time.

One last thought on this: Parents who ask questions are obviously seeking answers. They should feel free to write down the teacher's' responses so they can revisit the answers, reflect on them, and share some insights from the conference with their child. A good motto is: "The only dumb question is the one left unasked."

All questions are fair game. We should think about good and meaningful, open-ended questions, write them down, and be sure to ask them. The teachers really do want our questions to be answered.

"Where am I emotionally with regard to my ability to focus on my child?"

The Great Adventure can be an emotional roller coaster ride; especially if there is news a parent doesn't want to hear or she is dealing with a personal emotional situation at home. Emotions come in all kinds of packages and we must address a few of them here.

First and foremost, it is okay to cry. It's important to remember that we're not the first parents to feel overwhelmed and become emotional during a conference, and we certainly will not be the last. If a parent needs to excuse herself and then return to the conference, that is fine. If she is overwhelmed and needs to reschedule the appointment, that's also fine. She needs to let the teacher know that she will need her help with this situation. Sometimes, as a working parent or one who is going through other emotional times either with a spouse, another child, or an aging parent, the teacher's innocent question of "How are you?" may trigger an avalanche of tears. We may need to take a deep breath. We are all human. It's OK to ask for some support if we need to.

A second emotion to keep in check is anger. The conference may be short and we may not like the teacher or what the teacher has to say, however, anger will not open up communication. More specifically, as anger increases, the ability to hear important information about our child decreases. Even if we believe the teacher is an idiot, there is information about our child's day being conveyed. We need to keep focused on that fact. We do not have to be rude, disrespectful, or arrogant. We do not have to yell or call the teacher inappropriate names, even if we strongly disagree with the teacher. There is always another avenue to take. Besides, if a parent's reaction is "over the top" with anger, please believe me, teachers will be less likely to want to share information about a child directly with that parent. I am not saying teachers will be secretive about a child, but I am saying they are human and will be less likely to be eager to call the parent and openly share information in the future, even if it is good news. We need to keep ourselves (and our spouses, if necessary) in check.

I fully believe if there is a disagreement between a parent and a teacher about a child, it can be addressed respectfully. If the parent feels the need, an administrator, school psychologist, school social worker, guidance counselor, translator, or neutral teacher can all serve as a mediator so that a productive conference can be held. Every person involved with the child should feel comfortable to address and discuss concerns about that child. After all, we are the grown-ups, so all parties must participate and act appropriately regardless of the issues and keep the angry emotions in check.

Believe it or not, enthusiasm or excitement is another emotion we may need to keep in check. Something wonderful may be happening in our world, and just because the teacher's opening line is "How's life?" doesn't mean we need to reveal every detail. We are there to listen, discuss, and learn about our child. Our enthusiasm about our personal issues needs to be minimized so that the time we have to talk and learn about our child's educational life can be maximized.

"Am I doing most of the listening or the talking?"

The exchange between listening and talking defines a conversation. The two processes go hand in hand and both are critical for the transference of information. I am a believer that they cannot happen simultaneously. Generally speaking, the person doing the talking gives verbal information and the person listening receives the verbal information. Logically then, the parent in a conference about his child, should be doing more listening than speaking if his goal is to gain information. On the contrary, if the purpose of the conference is to give information about the child, then the parent should be doing most of the talking. It becomes clear that the role of listener or talker depends on the purpose of the conference. In most conferences, parents have an obligation and responsibility to do both—listen and talk.

A word of caution is necessary. I have been involved in hundreds of conferences by now, either personally or professionally. I can't tell you how often a parent starts chatting about her other children and the minutes on the classroom clock ticks by. Perhaps the teacher involved had an older child a few years ago, or a sibling is a celebrity of some sort. Regardless of the specifics, as the mother (usually) talks, time flies by. Suddenly, there is minimal time left to talk about the child the conference had been scheduled for. This will sound harsh, but the parent may need to say to herself a few times, "Shut up and listen." There is a time to talk and a time to listen. In the majority of conferences, it is essential that parents make sure their talking and listening processes are balanced and remain focused on the child everyone is there to discuss. The parent came to hear about this particular child of hers and how he or she is performing academically right now. She needs be careful not to dominate the time with "how beautifully the older one is doing now." Parents need to be cautious, and be sure to check in with themselves mentally during the conference by asking, "Am I doing most of the listening or talking?"

"Is the teacher as nervous as I am?"

We are complex individuals. How we function and react is a compilation of many factors that have been learned and reinforced over many years. Parents and teachers are often more similar than they are different.

They both bring their emotions, values, and experiences to the table at each conference. Many conferences start with a bit of uneasiness, but quickly slide into a comfortable dialogue. Quite rapidly, the parent and teacher relieve each other's concerns, and the exchange of information occurs smoothly. At other times this is not the case. The teacher and parent may remain in "high alert mode" throughout the conference. Each party continues to remain guarded during the conference. Sometimes the anxiety is so high anyone in the room can almost feel it. Other times, one comment or a simple body gesture can trigger the anxiety for either party. If this happens, they both might need to take a deep breath and remember the goal: open communication to gain and share important information about the child. Before a parent makes any judgments about the teacher, she should ask herself if the teacher seems as nervous as she does. If she is, then this may be an opportunity to explore the barriers that may be existing between the two parties, making all participants feel anxious. If this anxiety or nervousness interferes, communication may break down and the parent may not gain the information she needs about her child's academic performance.

Quite often, the teacher and the parent may be feeling rushed to either get home or get to work, depending on the time of day. Both have lives beyond the conference times, and both have feelings that may resemble "intimidation" or "anxiety." The parents are working off the experiences of the past, rumors they hear about the teacher, and concerns they may have regarding their child's performance and/or social interactions. The teacher is working off of past experiences or lack of conference experience, rumors he hears about the parents' reactions in the past, their perception or judgment of the parents' involvement, and the news they must deliver to the parents, especially if it is not very good news. This nervousness on both sides of the conversation can shut down communication, which is in complete contrast to what the goal should be. Acknowledgment of the possible anxiety must be realized and be dealt with either internally or externally so that the focus remains on the focus—the child.

"Is there respect around the table?"

I have often sat at the table as a parent wondering, "Who is this lady talking about?" At other times I have sat at the table as a teacher wondering "Who is this lady talking about?" It is obvious that the teacher and parent know the child in different, but equally important, ways.

At the parent-teacher conference, this difference of perspectives can become very obvious. The one thing that must be kept in the forefront of a parent's mind is that each person must be respectful of the perspectives being shared at the table. On the one side is the trained professional. She sees hundreds of children throughout the year, has passed mandated state tests that required her to do hundreds of hours of course work in educational theory, content, and law. She is supervised by an administrator and is obligated to understand normal childhood development and be responsible for the individual educational needs of every child in her class. On the other side of the table is the parent who loves this particular child more than anything else. She has brought this child into this world, taken responsibility for him, and has a strong desire for the best for her child academically, emotionally, and socially. She knows her child's fears and dreams and can give a detailed history of her child's short life on earth. She knows what makes her child laugh, cry, or become angry. She also knows her own fears for her child—some spoken and some forever silent in her heart.

These two individuals, sitting on opposite sides of the table, come together to discuss the same kid. *Wow.* A lot can happen here. As long as both parties acknowledge and respect the perspectives and experiences brought to the table by the other, communication and sharing can take place in order to maximize the child's performance. Together, an unbelievable team can collaborate to create an environment to best serve the child, but both sides must work together to fully respect the other, always keeping the child's best interest at the center of every conversation and action.

"Do I need to hear what the teacher is saying?"

Respect must be present for a productive conference to occur, but we all know we can fake it. It is possible to seem to respect someone by acting as though we are listening, when we are really working on a totally disconnected mental grocery list. We have all done this at one time or another.

Regardless of the dynamics between the teacher and ourselves, do we need to hear what the teacher is saying? This is a fair question and the only right answer is, yes, absolutely. We may not agree with what the teacher is saying, but we need to hear it for several reasons.

First and foremost, it is about our child, and it may be true. We need to hear it and deal with it. Second, it's what the teacher may be saying to other teachers about our child and we should know it. It is always inappropriate and unprofessional for a teacher to share information or opinions about a child to another parent, but it is often a professional responsibility for a teacher to share her perceptions and concerns about a child to other professionals within the building.

If it is an educational concern, a teacher may share it with other regular education teachers, special education teachers, the school nurse, the school psychologist, or the building administrator in order to seek strategies to use with the child. If it is an emotional or social concern, the school psychologist, school social worker, or guidance counselors are the appropriate professionals with whom the teacher should be discussing the child. Whether we agree or not, these educational or social concerns may be shared among the professionals for very legitimate reasons.

Third, the information may be how others in and around the school may be perceiving the child and the parent needs to know this so that he can help his child act and/or react appropriately to the verbal and nonverbal cues he may be receiving at school. An example here might be that your child's teacher tells you that several girls in the class are reporting to her that your ten-year-old daughter is being "bossy". The kids no longer want to play with her at recess. The teacher is trying to address it by having class discussions about assertive versus aggressive behaviors to help all of the students learn to take a proactive role with problem solving among their peers. This may surprise the parent that the teacher is reporting his angel as being bossy, because at home he only sees her as being quiet and withdrawn. This is a major piece of information that the parent needs to hear. This information, based on other kids' perceptions and filtered to the parent by the teacher, may help to explain why the parent's daughter is becoming more withdrawn. As the parent thinks about it, the fact that the phone has stopped ringing and his daughter's friends are "busy" each Saturday when she invites them over begins to make sense. This is critical information that the parent must use to help his daughter understand and analyze her social role with her peers.

This feedback—often something the parent doesn't want to hear, but must hear during conferences—is just information. Parents can choose what to do with it once they have heard it and reflected on it, but it is still just feedback or information. Parents should try to hear it with an open mind and consider when and how they want to deal with it.

"What do I do after the conference?"

What happens after the conference, matters. Suggestions, plans, and ideas will have been shared and, as a parent, if we have agreed with the issues and solution plan, we have a responsibility to carry through with them. Perhaps, we agreed that our child should read more at home or practice his math facts or stay after school each time he is rude to an adult. Whatever the plan is, it must be adhered to. No excuses! This is a commitment that we made and must adhere to as a role model to our child. (Reread Step 7!)

The parent, along with the teacher, has an obligation to implement and assess the strategies and continue to dialogue about the results of the strategies. These dialogues do not have to wait until the next formal conference date. Phone calls, emails, or good old-fashioned notes can be transmitted to each other to be sure progress is being made as a follow up to the conference discussions.

Another important piece of follow through is for parents to review the conference with their child. Even if he is in kindergarten, he can understand there was a conversation about his behavior and academic progress. Parents may have to bring the language down to a level he can understand, but it is a wonderful opportunity for parents and their child to discuss another person's perception of how he behaves and achieves at school. It can also open up the conversations about his day, his friends, his strengths and weaknesses, and his interests at school. These are valuable conversations to have. Parents need to exercise care, though. They don't need make this conference into something that is negative or demeaning to their child. The teacher should not be perceived as the "evil one," because this is the person the child spends six to seven hours with on a daily basis. If there is negative information to be conveyed and discussed, parents should do it in a manner that is productive. The feedback must always be shared with the child in a positive light.

- For example: If Johnny is mean to classmates, the parent has a choice when she discusses this with Johnny.

- She can say, "Why are you so mean to everyone? Do you think anyone will like if you do that? I don't want to get any calls from that teacher about this? Do you understand me?"

- Or she can say, "Your teacher really cares about you. She told me sometimes you have some trouble with working out a problem with your classmates. What's going on? When there's trouble and you feel like being mean, what can you do? Your teacher and I agreed that she is going to call me the next time you are mean to another kid, so that we can talk about it. I asked her to do this because I need to know you are at school learning, not being mean to others. Do you understand this plan?"

The parent-teacher conference quite often is a formal starting point for many open and informal discussions about a child's performance. Both teacher and parent have the responsibility to keep the lines of communication open, and the obligation to follow through so that the child makes academic, social, and emotional progress.

"What if I don't feel satisfied after a conference?"

If a conference goes in a direction that feels unproductive to the parent, or if it ends and the parent feels unsatisfied, he has the parental responsibility to take the right steps to address his concerns. He has an obligation to his child that his concerns are heard and addressed appropriately. It's not good enough to be angry and upset and then stay that way. A parent shouldn't go around town badmouthing that "lousy, good-for-nothing teacher who doesn't even know what she is doing."

A responsible parent will take proactive steps to help his child, if the child is not being served appropriately. However, this also implies that the parent is being reasonable about his child as a part of a public school system. If the system is giving its fair share to give an appropriate education to the child, then so be it. If the parent feels unsatisfied after careful reflection, then he must take appropriate steps to resolve his concerns. That's what grownups do, and this is what a parent must do to ensure they are on the right path to raising a healthy and well-educated child.

I will state openly that I believe every public school has a handbook. If I'm not 100 percent correct, please forgive me because I am probably pretty close. Parents should read it and understand what is in it. It is a public document so everybody can know what the rules of the game are. If a parent feels dissatisfied with the results of a conference, he can go to this document first, see what steps are listed there, and then follow them. That may be a tough step to take, but parents need to follow the procedures spelled out for everyone. These are the established "rules of the game."

Most schools will tell parents to start at the teacher level when they believe there is a problem. Following a conference, therefore, an appropriate step might be for the parent to request a second conference to clear up concerns. He may have to use a support staff member, but that's why they are part of the system. There may be a guidance counselor, social worker, school nurse, or psychologist who can help clarify concerns or attend the second conference with the parent so everyone can stay focused on the child and not get distracted and off task because of emotions. This is an appropriate step and should be viewed as a viable option.

If this still is unproductive, administrators are available at the building level and at the district level. Remember, the goal is to solve the problem at the lowest level of conflict. Parents need to make sure they are following the right path to solve their questions, though. If they jump right to the superintendent and the board of education members over a relatively simple issue, they will send you right back to the building level. And they should. It is only at the building level that day-to-day concerns can be addressed and plans implemented with the people who work most closely with the child. Parents need to keep their child as their focus. In addition, parents should remember that teachers are human. If a parent becomes known as one who runs to the "higher bosses" over perceived incidental things, people will be less eager to want to work with that parent and her child. It is human nature. Teachers will become leery of the parent's motives, reluctant to call her in to discuss relatively small issues involving her child, and become defensive in her presence. It is a natural self-protection mode when a perceived threatening situation is upon us. It also completely shuts down open and honest communication about the child.

My advice here is, in every school district, as with every business, there is a chain of command. Parents should become familiar with the one in their school district and use it if they need to. They should follow the procedures that are outlined and published (usually in the school handbook) by the system so that the system can work with them as they strive to always benefit their children's education.

In this section, I've brought up some common concerns and questions about the Great Adventure of parent-teacher conferencing that I have heard and lived through. Embedded in this section is heartfelt advice for managing emotions during these conferences. I've also reflected on my personal experiences as a mother being on the "other side of the table." We are all humans who are madly in love with our offspring. We want the best for them, and the parent-teacher conference can be a powerful tool by which information is shared.

Before your next parent-teacher conference, take a deep breath, reflect on the following questions, and honestly look into your heart for your true answers.

Ask yourself:

1. *What are my personal feelings about school?*

2. *When do I ask for a conference?*

3. *What communication skills do I need?*

4. *What questions should I ask?*

5. *Where am I emotionally with regard to my ability to focus on my child?*

6. *Am I doing most of the listening or the talking?*

7. *Is the teacher as nervous as I am?*

8. *Is there respect around the table?*

9. *Do I need to hear what the teacher is saying?*

10. *What do I do after the conference?*

11. *What if I don't feel satisfied after a conference?*

Part III:

A Middle School Kid Moved in Last Night

Remember the first time your baby looked at you and said, "No"? Remember the first time your child and you "argued" about picking up his clothes, or not slamming the cup into the sink? And you thought, "Hmm, will this matter in ten years?" It seemed so far away. Guess what? Ten years flies by, and now your baby is off to middle school. It seems like all you did was blink your eyes for a second and the time went by. Parents will agree that they have had this same experience. It seems like time flashed before their eyes and yet, at the same time, when they watch their adolescent's behavior it sometimes seems like no time has passed. In fact, it may feel like that same egocentric two-year-old "brat" is still there. In a strange way, she is.

As our children struggle through childhood and into adolescence, the egocentricity returns. They have learned that they can separate from us, not see us, and yet know that we still exist (kindergarten age). They have learned that rules exist, we take turns, and other people's feelings count (elementary age), and yet, lo and behold, that egocentric view comes back as they begin to ask the question and figure out "Who am I?" This is every child's job as he continues to grow and learn throughout the adolescent years.

The middle school years are a time of transition. For children, every day can seem like a new transition. Their bodies change before their eyes, their own voices may not sound familiar to them, and people expect more from them. An adolescent could end up feeling as if every day is a new and strange experience. As we know, transitions, or times of change, are difficult for some adults to handle. Rare is the adolescent who sails through this time of transition unscathed. As the adults in charge of these newfound amoebas, it is our job to help them understand themselves. Not an easy task.

When everything seems bizarre with this unfamiliar creature we need to look deeply into its eyes if we can, or stare at it for approximately five minutes while it is sleeping. We will see that needy tender baby somewhere deep in the body of this strange sleeping giant. Our baby really is there, it's just that the middle school kid has taken over his body. We need to have fun during this time. We'll never experience anything else quite like it.

As our adolescents move into our homes, we will take a look at parenting in a whole new light. This is an exciting time in the life of parenting. We'll need to keep our sense of humor, above all else. We'll be living with a funny creature at this time in life, and we won't want to miss it. Our daughter's, or son's, logic will suck and yet somehow sound reasonable as she or he says it with a straight face. I'm going to say it again. We'll need to keep our sense of humor, above all else.

I've limited myself to ten definite concepts to keep in mind always when dealing with middle school kids. Honestly though, there are probably hundreds more to think about. These concepts are in no specific order. The true parental challenge is to keep these all in mind simultaneously.

Concept 1—We all love and want the best for our children.

I do not believe that there is a parent out there who would not do everything in his power for his child in a time of need. There is nothing that can compare to a parent's love for his or her child. Sometimes it is very hard to take a step back and watch our child struggle even though we know in our heart that this struggle will allow our children to grow into stronger people. Logically, we know we must do this, but emotionally, it is difficult. As hard as it seems, it is so important to stick with our logical side, not our emotional side, when these times arise.

Here's a good example. Your thirteen-year-old daughter is invited to the graduation party of the most popular eighth-grade girl. All the boys and girls she grew up with will be there. You've done everything right. You've called the house and the mother (a friend of yours now after all the shared experiences of elementary and middle school) will be home. She assures you that the twenty-five invited kids will be down in the basement, and she plans on taking a walk downstairs every hour or so. Your daughter is "dying to go."

Uh-oh. You love her and want the best for her. Now what? The choice is yours. Let her go? Offer to help chaperone the party? Talk to your friend about the risks of having twenty-five unsupervised adolescents in her basement? Risk sounding like an overprotective prude? Your daughter begins the begging and crying routine and using great logic, i.e., "We won't drink. What's the worst we can do, make out? So-and-so's mother trusts us, why can't you?" Your daughter's emotions swing from a calm woman-to-woman discussion to a full-blown "hissy fit."

Your emotional heart breaks for her, while your logical mind knows you need to keep her safe, but allow her to grow. There are some logical, good, and sensible steps you can take. The trick is to remain rational while figuring out a safe and acceptable agreement. Some ideas may include offering to chaperone and then doing it. Perhaps, offer her an alternative to the party; maybe a special family treat she's been waiting for. Maybe you can provide her with a cell phone to call her every half-hour or have her call you if she needs you. (Here is a special side caution I must interject regarding cell phones and adolescents. Although cell phones allow you to contact your child at any moment, they also allow your child not to be where you think he or she is. Our children, with cell phones, can tell us they are in one place when in reality they can call from any place. Trust, discussion, and honesty go hand in hand with cell phones. Building trust, having discussions, and relying on honesty needed to start ten years ago to ensure their trust, honesty, and reliability at age fourteen.)

Back to the logical decision you must make with your child regarding the "popular girl's party." There's no easy answer, sorry. You need to know in your heart what is right for you and your child, feel comfortable with your decision, and then make the best out of the situation.

We will see the "best of our brat" shine through as they struggle to move through adolescence. Most of it is a phase. By going back and thinking about our parenting decisions when our children were two years old, and how we handled various behaviors during that phase, we may be able to revert to some common ground with them and come to a mutual understanding. Humor is a must. Flexible guidelines and structured boundaries can also get us through most situations. Sometimes, however, a highly qualified individual, such as a counselor, therapist, or psychologist may be necessary for us and/or our children. Either we, as the parents, our children, or all of us together may need the guidance of a certified professional to create the necessary environment for open and honest communication. This professional may also offer strategies to ease difficult times, such as the previous example and opportunities to reflect on each other's emotional needs. These professionals are available for long or short-term needs, in every community. Use your pediatrician, the school psychologist, or your local phone book to locate a certified professional you feel comfortable with to help you through the challenging communication times.

Even though we love our adolescents and we want the best for them, at this time in their lives, we may not be able to understand everything about them.

Their logic and emotions may collide, but our hearts and minds must stay focused.

Concept 2—Teachers and parents are here to help a child learn from his own experiences.

Teachers and parents are here to help a child to learn from his own experiences. This does not mean we must nag the child constantly, but it does mean we must take time to help him process the numerous experiences he has with him, so that he can fully benefit from the experiences he has. Most adolescents need help to process the world going on around them and within themselves. The adolescent mind is absorbing and sorting out all kinds of information constantly. Any given middle school child will directly interact with approximately ten to fifteen different adults and a minimum of fifty to one hundred peers on a typical day, if he is in a public school.

The information, comments made, judgments passed, and feedback given all are filtered through their five senses and brought to a very busy mind: a hub of never-ending activities. Teachers and parents can help sort out the relevant from the irrelevant information and help the child to delete meaningless information through a strategy I call "the mirror effect." By asking questions back at her (like a reflecting glass), an adolescent has the opportunity to think and process information, formulate ideas, and attach meaning to the pieces of information. This is an ongoing process. It doesn't occur in a split second or even overnight. But it is an important process. For any given incident, these questions might sound like: Who was there? How did she handle the situation? What made her react that way? What evidence is there that this might be true? What was your reaction? Why does that reaction seem fair? What would the incident look like from an outsider's view? There are literally hundreds of questions that can help a child analyze a situation, reflect on his involvement in a situation, and learn something from the incident. By using "the mirror effect" we are modeling appropriate thought processes to help our child analyze a situation and attach valuable meaning to it. This is an important life long skill.

Regardless of how we give feedback, the more love we can show through our actions and words, the better. Remember, these are emotional and sometimes illogical and irrational creatures we're dealing with. If we can tap some of that emotional energy, the impact can be powerful and our words may be brought to a deeper processing point in the kid's mind. Middle school kids are funny creatures. Their egocentric attitude and mindset may indicate a need for some assistance from us to provide some clarity about their experiences as they grow. We must be sure to not overlook the lessons grounded in the experiences that abound them.

Quite frankly, the adolescent is bombarded with information coming back at them, but sometimes they can't make sense of it all. We, the adults in their lives, must be willing to listen openly, speak honestly, and help sort out the information and process it with them. We can reword content information, verbalize emotions, and put names and words onto situations. By talking about what is happening inside and outside of themselves, they can learn to reflect on experiences and evaluate situations for themselves. They can create options, make decisions, and categorize experiences with a certain amount of accuracy and self-confidence if they have been given opportunities to apply their skills and knowledge to their experiences. This is all a part of "growing up."

Concept 3—Adolescents learn from every experience—good, bad, and neutral.

Mistakes can be a good thing. Mistakes allow us to be challenged mentally and emotionally. Mistakes force us to assess our behaviors and critically analyze the situation occurring around us. This is true for adults, adolescents, and children. If it weren't for the many trials and errors that we all go through, I dare say none of us would figure out how to problem solve and resolve our own issues. For our adolescents' sake, sometimes we need to be their biggest cheerleader or most critical partner to help them grow from every experience. Concept 3 goes hand in hand with Concept 2.

Sometimes, bad experiences must happen so that the deeper, more meaningful life lesson can be revealed. In times like these, we may have to remind ourselves that there is a life lesson buried somewhere in the moment. A perfect example may be when one of our children is suspended for plagiarizing. The moment of suspension is not a joyous one; however, the life lesson regarding honesty, trust, hard work, and the legal issues around plagiarizing are the very real life lessons to be learned. We need to take a deep breath and look for the bigger life lessons. It's not easy, but it is critical.

Not all mistakes have to be someone's fault either. A bombed math test, could be the teacher's fault for not teaching the concepts thoroughly enough, or the kid's fault for not studying enough. It could also just be an aberration that occurred and now can be processed with guidance and love. It is simply an experience whereby the events leading to it can be analyzed, the follow-up or reaction steps can be planned, and the child can learn that Mom and Dad still love him and everyone is still breathing normally after a "bump in the road" with a math test.

On the other hand, a bigger conversation must take place, and deeper analysis must occur if "the bombed math test" is not a unique event but rather a part of a pattern. Maybe something else is happening and a pattern or downward spiral is occurring. This is an absolutely necessary time to look critically at what's going on in and around the relationship between our children and us. Our expectations, involvement, communication, and interactions need to be looked at and perhaps modified in some way. Again, mistakes happen. The critical question is where does it fit into the bigger picture? Is it a simple event, or a part of an emerging pattern? After careful fact finding, thoughtful reflection, and critical analysis of the situation, the parent and child, must decide. If it is a part of a much bigger picture or we need assistance to flesh out the incidences and their meanings, then so be it. We can get help. The school, a local church, or public community center can help direct us to someone who is available to assist us. But, we must take the necessary action steps to help our children learn from life experiences and make progress towards adulthood successfully. Again, every experience is a learning opportunity. What we choose to do with the experience is what continues to matter ten years from now.

Concept 4—Finding a balance regarding a newfound need for privacy is critical.

Adolescence is a time of learning and stretching the boundary lines of independence. Just as our children needed to learn how to separate from us when they were young, they will need to go through a similar process as an adolescent. To do this, they must rely on themselves to make decisions and think about options. They may share these options and decisions with their friends, but not us. We shouldn't take it personally. Understand that it is a necessary part of growing up. We can think back to when we were thirteen or so. We didn't tell our parents everything. And we probably hated when they asked us about our private thoughts and activities. Most of what we did during our day was not discussed. Sure, we placated our parents with the usual topics around school coursework maybe, but very few of us shared our emotions or insecurities about ourselves and our friends openly at the dinner table. We may have appeared aloof or withdrawn to our parents. But to our adolescent self, it was just private. It was our own business that we were working on privately. This is exactly the feeling our adolescents have going on internally during this time. It's their personal and private matters that they are dealing with. It's their personal business. They need to be given the opportunity to work things out for themselves so that ultimately they believe in their capabilities as new situations and challenges arise. In general, a good rule of thumb is to give them the space and privacy they need so that they can grow. Allow them to amaze you!

On the other hand, privacy can sometimes become a big issue and a parental challenge. Often it can be a big issue because the minute we try to understand it we are accused by our adolescent that we're butting in. It is tempting to want to know something as soon as we're told we can't. And quite honestly, our minds begin to wander and conjure up all kinds of scary scenarios involving the kids in our homes who won't tell us anything. The harsh fact is in reality, it may not be any of our business. It is personal, and most personal business is private. This fact can frustrate many parents, but I would venture to say, the typical adolescent is not "hiding" anything. He is simply learning to incorporate information from the world, ponder it, and make sense of it. The privacy issue comes into play while he tries to separate and live within the expectations that have been established for him. This type of thinking, though, begs the question: When does healthy normal privacy cross a line into unhealthy, perhaps even dangerous, privacy?

As hard as it might be for us, at some points, our children deserve some privacy, just as every healthy adult strives for some privacy daily. Privacy does not have to equal secrecy though. From a parental standpoint, privacy should be respected; however, secrecy must be explored. If there is something at a gut level for us, and our intuition is telling us there is something about our children's behavior, friends, or attitudes, to be worried about, this is not the time to respect our children's secretive natures. If the phone rings, we pick up, and the caller immediately hangs up or won't give his/her name or if our child repeatedly drops the screen on the computer every time we enter the room, our gut should tell us to take a look at what is going on. We may need some help with understanding this, and we may have to seek it from the professionals who are right there in our community who are willing to help. We should talk to our adolescents about the changes in their behavior, attitude, and friends, but try hard to respect their requests for privacy. This is a fine line we are walking. Our adolescents are going through some fast and serious changes: emotionally, physically, and mentally. They need to get to know themselves as new people. They want to explore their independence and yet they need to know we are there to support them when they need help. We must talk and model privacy, but also encourage and engage in common time with our children. We will be amazed at the new adult who is emerging from his private cocoon.

Concept 5—Networking with other parents to better understand our children's lives is critical.

While trying to accept the private nature of the child you used to share every moment with, networking with other parents to better understand your child's life is critical. This may be your best survival technique while you are dealing with the adolescent living in your house. Ways of networking and understanding your new adolescent may include (but are not limited to in any way):

- Stay close to your "girlfriends" and "neighbors" with similar aged children.

- Talk to parents of other adolescents.

- As tired as you are, go to the PTO meetings at the middle school and high school every chance you get.

- Sit, be still, and listen to other parents talk at the football game, before the soccer match, or in the auditorium before the holiday concerts. Listen to what they talk about. Undoubtedly, you will hear comments about "what their kid told them," when the science fair is going to be held, what happened at the last school dance, etc....

- For some reason, parents feel a strong need to know everything about the elementary school teachers and activities, but this need drops dramatically as the years go by. However, it may be even more critical for you to be very involved as your child moves through the secondary levels of schooling. Research tells us that students of parents, who remain active and communicate regularly with the schools, do better academically. Besides all that, and perhaps even more importantly, these little tidbits you pick up can serve as a springboard into conversations with your child. Using these little tidbits, you will probably get more information or at least an opening into a conversation by saying, "Mrs. So and So was telling me about the bus ride on the field trip" rather than asking, "How was the field trip?" (9 out of 10 times you'll hear, "fine" and nothing more).

- Stay tuned in.

- Continue networking.

- Listen (or eavesdrop) always. It is important for you to hear what is going on in your child's world, since the move towards independence and the rules of privacy are in full swing.

This may look like just another rambling "TO DO" List, but in actuality they are strategies to try, in various combinations, to keep connected to your adolescent's life; the same adolescent who will continue to try to become increasingly private and independent. Keep in mind, as frustrating and difficult as it can be to rely on information from others and get nothing from your child, your adolescent needs to go through this to become a successful and capable adult.

Concept 6—Adolescents still need rules, boundaries, and love.

As much as most adolescents want to believe they are now more like an adult and should be treated as such, they are not. There is a very insecure side to all the bravado of adolescence, and every adolescent still feels safer when the boundaries are put around them. I am not saying we have to cage them in. In fact, it is my true belief that the reins will, and should be, naturally released to a certain extent; however, there still needs to be rules and boundaries that are supportive and clear.

Remember, privacy is to be respected, but secrecy is to be explored (see Concept 4). We need to know what they are doing, where they are going, and who they are with. We need to know who else will be there, who is "dropping off" and who is "picking up." They need to know our expectations with clear and concise language. They also need to know that there are consequences should the rules be broken. This does not start when they are eleven, twelve, or thirteen years old. Guess what. It should have started ten years ago.

Rules, boundaries, and love go hand in hand. We need to tell our adolescents we love them, every chance we get. The insecure thirteen-year old, as cool as he thinks he is, still needs to be sure that he is loved. We can tell him, show him, and be a model of love for him. Our adolescent son will thank us, when he is fully secure and confident in the man he has become. It takes time and patience. We need to continue to set expectations and boundaries because we love our teenager, and we need to tell them that this is why the boundaries are there. They may say they hate it, but they still need it. Remind them frequently that our number one responsibility is to keep them as safe as possible whenever possible, even when we are not standing right beside them.

Another important thing that comes into play here is that we allow ourselves to be the "fall guy." We should allow our children to use us as an excuse for not going along with the crowd anytime they want. We can be the bad guy that takes the blame. Here is an example. A child is at a friend's house. The parent knows where she is and has done all the "right" things to make sure she is safe. But, her friends now want to go to someplace else—a place the child knows her mother will not approve of. If the child has her mother's permission to use her as the bad guy, it gives her an out. It is okay if she says, "My mom is unstable and she'll go nuts if I even call her about this idea. You've never seen her lose her mind like I have." Another optional statement might be, "My mom is such a witch. She'll never say yes and she'll kill me if I go without her permission." These statements may not get her completely off of the peer-pressure hook, but what it can do for her is at least give her some way of trying to persuade her friends without having to take the heat all on her own. She can try to save face with her friends and stay safe at the same time. She's made her mom the bad guy, and that's OK. The goal is to keep her safe. We need to give our adolescents permission to use us.

The bottom line is, society has rules and boundaries for all of us as a way of keeping a civilized society and as an attempt to keep us all safe from harm. Our children need to know, from a very early age and throughout adolescence, that rules are a part of life. Rules never really go away and, ultimately, we are all responsible for each other's safety. We, as parents, can add love to the mix. Someday, our children will thank us for it. That day may be tomorrow or ten years from now.

Concept 7—Understand the conflicting messages that surround adolescents every day.

Conflicting messages surround us all. Conflicting messages about sex, language, TV, music, and social situations bombard our adolescents. They are told one thing; they see another. A friend, one day, betrays them the next. On the third day, they betray a different friend without setting out to do so. It is all very confusing. Their bodies are telling them one thing and their parents' voices, in their head, tell them something else. They are in a time in their lives where they are seeing injustices but are unsure of what to do about them. Be patient with them. Not many of us would choose to relive our adolescent years because it was so emotionally conflicting to us. They will pass through this period of life and look back on it as a time of growth, but while they are in the moment, they are going to need us to be the stabilizing factor in their unstable world.

As parents, we will need to help our adolescents process and understand these conflicting messages whenever the opportunity arises. If the opportunities don't arise, at least understand that they are faced with all of this information and may just need some quiet space to try to sort it all out. This is where necessary privacy comes in. Sometimes, just by making statements aloud i.e. "War is difficult to understand when we all know that most people in the world want to live in peace." can help them understand that we all have to deal with the inconsistencies of the messages and information that surrounds us. Knowing also that they don't have to engage in a conversation about it also helps them to simply think about it and try to process it.

No doubt about it, our adolescents are confused—inside and out—emotionally, physically, and intellectually. It is part of "growing up," and the reality is that there is nothing we can do as parents that can ease the confusing nature of life for our children. Even if we try to keep our adolescent in a bubble to reduce all outside conflicts as a way of shielding him from any unnecessary pain, the conflicts come from within as well. Our sons want to be "grown up," but we will catch them still playing with Legos. Our daughters will want us to respect them and allow them to wear "grown-up" clothing, and yet they can't part with their dolls that their Grandma gave them when they were six years old. As a matter of fact, they may still sleep with their dolls. Hormones will suddenly stir our daughter's body and make her notice that the geek next door, who she has known her whole life, is actually quite handsome. But why wasn't he cute yesterday? These emotions are real and very confusing and we can't protect our child from them. Nor should we even try. These conflicting emotions force adolescents to think, become aware, and learn from what's going on around them, inside and out.

We, as parents, can stand back and watch. It is an amazing process and should not be missed by the outsider. We should help where we can and talk when we must, but most importantly, we need to listen always. Sometimes, silence is the best thing we can offer our children. Our words may actually, and perhaps unintentionally, cause even greater conflicts at times. Simply understand that the conflicting messages are there and our children's mental and emotional processes are working overtime. So relax and observe. It's fascinating.

Concept 8—Adolescents are independent citizens who need to fit into the social world around them.

Hopefully, a long time ago, we, as parents, have asked ourselves, "What kind of adult do I want to raise?" The preferable answer had something to do with "one who can cope with life" and "one who will be a productive citizen in our world."

Well, guess what? The adults we've been hoping to raise are beginning to emerge. When we look at our adolescent sitting at our table showing his kid brother how to make obnoxious noises come from his cupped right hand under his left armpit, there will be glimmers of a wonderful citizen who is productive and able to cope. We need to keep the hope alive in our heart. Somehow this kid will fit into society. He is working on it.

Actually, at this point in time, adolescents are working overtime at becoming a part of society. We may not believe this, as we take a look at the lump that has been lying on the couch with the remote control all day, but it is true. Their minds and bodies are continuously managing a multitude of factors. Two of the most challenging questions they ask themselves, either consciously or subconsciously (while, perhaps, seeming, unconsciously), is "Who am I?" and "How do I fit in?" The questions may be worded differently, perhaps, as, "Who are my friends?" or "Would anyone miss me if I disappeared?" These questions fall under the social umbrella.

The social umbrella is broad and encompasses all of us. Our children really are vying for their position under the social umbrella. Our adolescent is actually trying to process the world around him and figure out exactly where he fits in. He may or may not like the answers he comes up with. Remember, he is a confused creature trying to figure out so many things simultaneously. He will either figure it out silently or with our feedback. But remember, maturity happens.

We can help our adolescents move along the continuum of determining their place in the world by helping where we can and accepting where our help is not needed. We can often help by talking, listening, and commenting on the world around them in a constructive manner, instead of judging their comments or observations. We can probe them for their ideas and provide them with a sounding board for their answers. We can also help by knowing when to seek professional support for them if need be.

Sometimes just talking to an "unaffiliated outsider" can be helpful for any of us. Many adults use this technique, whether it is a professional therapist or a close confidant who will be honest, open, and fair. This holds true for adolescents as well. Encourage them to seek advice from any appropriate adult in their world—a guidance counselor, school social worker, the school nurse, an administrator, or a favorite teacher all can serve as a great sounding board for our children. In addition, these professionals are often more than willing to talk to parents, in order to help them understand the scary world of the adolescent mind. If a parent feels she needs a sounding board or some validation with regard to her child's growth and social development, she should never hesitate to contact the school. These trained professionals probably have a collective number of years that are in the hundreds. If need be, parents should use them and learn from their experiences so they can help their child grow. The school professionals will also help them determine if their child is "off the mark." In this case, they can often help parents learn about what community resources are available to them and their child. As part of the school system, these professionals are always willing, ready, and able to assist teens and parents so that a solid and socially healthy adult can emerge from the emotional and developing adolescent creature.

The goal is to help our adolescents understand where they fit under the social umbrella as an independent citizen. Our job is to help them find this understanding.

Concept 9—Adolescents must become self-advocates by practicing conflict resolution at the lowest possible level.

By now you have realized (if you didn't know it already) that parenting is an awesome career. It is not a "day job," "night job," or "summer job." There is not a clock to punch, no breaks, and no holidays off. Parenting is a full-time career choice. It is also is a complex and ever-changing challenge. Static and boring are two terms never associated with it. There are layers of work to be done in order for a socially and emotionally healthy adult to arrive into society ready to cope with whatever life throws at him or her. As parents, we are the creators and directors of these beings. We are the facilitators and coaches who strive for success. At a certain point in time, we will step back and watch a beautiful person advocate for herself with confidence and competence. For competence to develop, skills need to be taught. For confidence to develop, practice and evaluation of the application of the skills must occur. We've been practicing with both a little at a time during this person's whole life. Adolescence will be filled with opportunities, perhaps daily, for us to practice teaching this creature how to advocate for herself and resolve her own personal issues with confidence and competence.

To this end, an extremely important job we have as parents of an adolescent is knowing when to step in and when to stay out. Quite honestly, sometimes it is a guessing game. A crying, whining, "falling apart" kid may only want us to listen to his venting, but would be devastated if we took action. When in doubt, we should ask our children what it is they want us to do. The answer may surprise us when they say, "Nothing." Then, we should do nothing and let them resolve their own conflicts, if they can. We should, however, always let them know we are there as a sounding board, guide, or advocate, if the need arises.

This is a time in an adolescent's life when the challenge becomes being a self-advocate. He is taking ownership of all kinds of situations and therefore must take the responsibility to take action to solve his own problems. He has been learning many social skills, and listening to and watching the adults around him. Now is the time these adolescents must take the necessary action steps to affect their world. They may be faced with a problem or new plan of action. Of course, a great way to help them prepare for this is to role play or talk through various scenarios with them, but the job of taking action belongs to them, and it needs to remain with them. We need to trust our instincts and the lessons we've given them along the way. They can resolve many issues on their own now, before they escalate and need our involvement. We should step back and let them take control of their own lives in small ways first, letting them handle a conflict with their friend or a poor grade with a teacher. We can allow them to speak up for themselves at the clothes shop or ask for assistance at the courtesy desk in the grocery store. These are little developmental experiences leading to a critical step toward independence. If we let them experience success with small competencies initially, confidence will continue to increase with every positively reinforced opportunity.

We need to have confidence in our children's social abilities that we have nurtured over the past ten years, so they can have confidence in their own social abilities for the next ten years. Our children will amaze us, if we let them.

Concept 10—Parents are the number one role model for their adolescent at all times.

We are the number one role model for our children, at all times. That is an awesome, powerful, and perhaps, scary thought. What an incredible responsibility. How we handle life, relationships, and stress will be repeated through our children. We may have to wait anywhere from ten minutes to forty years, but we will see ourselves in our children's ability to handle life, relationships, and stress. Sometimes, if there are issues that we are trying to deal with for ourselves, looking back to our own parents to understand ourselves can be beneficial. Our children will do the same someday and wonder, "What would Mom or Dad do in this situation?" The hope is they'll have enough skills gathered in their repertoire that they learned from us to weigh the facts and possible outcomes and then determine the best way for themselves to handle the issues.

Remember the old adage, "It's not what you say, but what you do that matters." Even if we don't want to always admit it, there is truth in that statement. Our children are watching us—the good, the bad, and the ugly parts of what we do. They are watching how we speak to the school teachers and how we speak and act toward our spouses. They are watching how we care for the elderly and how we respect individual differences among our neighbors. Our children are mentally recording everything we say and do. It's important to talk to our adolescent children about the choices we make, but more importantly we should role model good choices for them always.

The very important bottom line is to remember to love this adolescent creature and model love always. The adolescent may not understand or appreciate all we do, but she will come to appreciate our demonstrations of love and our efforts to help her through adolescence. She is a strange creature living at home right now. She is not sure of what she is supposed to be thinking and doing. She is even surprising herself sometimes with her own thoughts and actions. She needs her parents, and really does love them. She's just lost her mind for a little while, but she will be back.

As our children grow, develop, and emerge into adults, our relationship with them will change. Initially it may seem that it is changing in a bad way, but ultimately, the relationship will grow in a very healthy way. As our adolescent matures, our relationship will also mature. As we think back to our own middle school years, almost each of us, if we are really honest with ourselves, will remember a time where we believed our parents didn't understand anything about our life. Now the shoe is on the other foot, as the saying goes. Our children, at this age, truly believe we don't have a clue, but it is our job to help guide them, love them, and stay clued into what is going on during this critical developmental stage. That's why these ten concepts are so important to keep in mind.

1. *We all love and want the best for our children.*

2. *Teachers and parents are here to help a child learn from his own experiences.*

3. *Adolescents learn from every experience—good, bad, and neutral.*

4. *Finding a balance regarding a newfound need for privacy is critical.*

5. *Networking with other parents to better understand our children's lives is critical.*

6. *Adolescents still need rules, boundaries, and love.*

7. *Understand the conflicting messages that surround adolescents.*

8. *Adolescents are becoming independent citizens who need to fit into the social world.*

9. *Adolescents must become self-advocates by practicing conflict resolution at the lowest possible level.*

10. *Parents are the number one role model for their adolescents at all times.*

These concepts are not the only golden rules for thinking about adolescents, but they are key thoughts to keep in mind. Our adolescents will challenge us daily and stretch our parental skills beyond our wildest imaginations—but this is their job. They must keep us on our toes; and we must always stay one toe ahead of them. Our relationship will seem strained at times. This is normal. Our friendship with them may weaken at times. This is normal. Our desire to be with them may vary from one minute to the next. And this too is normal. Adolescent development during the middle school years does this to us. It keeps us being in the middle—somewhere between parent and friend, understanding and confusion, all-knowing and completely unbalanced.

We can have fun with it. This age group is wonderful and perplexing to watch firsthand. They are amazing creatures. Their abilities will shock and befuddle us—sometimes at the very same time.

The middle school years are intriguing years and they really do only last a few years. We need to keep it in perspective. Even when our children really tick us off with a bad attitude or random rude behavior, we need to try hard to remember that somewhere behind the pimples and greasy hair is a beautiful butterfly waiting to break free from its awkward cocoon. If we have laid the foundation over the past twelve to sixteen years, a beautiful young adult will emerge from that middle school adolescent. We need to be there and be vigilant. It would be a shame to not see it happen. We don't want to miss it.

Part IV:

The Big Scary World

The world can be a scary place and it is our job as parents to raise young adults who can cope with whatever comes their way. This is a monumental task. When talking about when we were young, many of us say things such as "My parents would have killed me if they ever got called into the school because of my behavior." or "My parents would never have called the principal to ask him to change my team or class teacher." or, "My parents couldn't have cared less if I wasn't in the same class with my friends. As a matter of fact, they probably wrote a note and asked the school to separate us from any of my friends."

Some of these phrases may sound familiar. Maybe you can add a few more of your own. The bottom line is, many of the parents of the generation before saw the value of having their babies struggle a little in life. They certainly didn't want to see great pain being inflicted upon us; however, they often would wait before rushing in to save us. My experience has shown me that we, today's parents, often want our babies to be "happy" and "feel good." However, it is hard to know "happy" until we've had a little "sad," and "feeling good" often arrives right after "working through a challenging situation and feeling successful in the end." Sometimes it's important to pause before taking action for our child. Our child needs to experience a range of challenges if he is to develop the necessary skills to deal effectively with the Big Scary World.

Educators would say that true learning comes through some struggle. And ultimately we all really do feel better about ourselves when we have realized we accomplished something we didn't believe we could. So, if this is true, and that is my belief through my professional experiences, then why is it that today's parents want to "fix things" so quickly so their baby (or toddler or child or adolescent) won't have to struggle through it. This generation of parents should be careful not to enable their children into a place where they don't believe they can solve their own problems and come out stronger in the end. We need to consider the fact that our need to immediately act on behalf of our children will set our children up so they will not be able to act on their own behalf with confidence.

Our children learn from their experiences and our interactions with them. To prepare them for the "big scary world" we must plan our course of action at least ten years in advance. Let's take a look at the necessary skills for managing life in the "big scary world."

When a child, either young or a teen, has an outburst, either verbal or physical, because he does not get his own way or he is frustrated by the situation, a couple of things could be going on. First, the child could have a legitimate emotional instability happening whereby professional help must be sought. Or second, the child may have not yet learned how to cope with what life presents to him. Far too often, in my experience, the latter of these two is often true. When I ask myself, "Where should these coping skills come from?" my most solid answer is undeniably, "His parents." This is our job in life, and it instantly came with the turf of parenthood.

When a child does not learn the necessary coping skills, scary things can happen. Risky behaviors can rise to the surface and may take the shape of drug or alcohol use, and inappropriate sexual activity. As a child learns to break free into independence she learns these coping skills. As the young adolescent carefully examines her world, she tests these skills. These coping skills involve a host of labels, but they are commonly identified as listening, processing, clarification, problem-solving, and self-advocacy skills.

Listening is different than hearing. It involves more than just the ears. Listening implies an active brain. It implies that body language is being assessed, while nonverbal cues and tone of voice are being processed. It implies that the context is being embedded into the words as the listener is listening. When an individual is "listening," hearing, thinking, and comprehending occur simultaneously. Listening is a very complex process. It needs to be practiced, reflected upon, and fine-tuned throughout life.

Processing is the actual steps that occur when meaning is being applied to sounds and images inside the head of an individual. These skills may work quickly in one child's head and more slowly in another child's. (The same is true for adults, by the way.) These abilities may be fully intact or impaired in some way. They may also be encouraged and reinforced by the feedback the child gets about his or her own processing of information. As adults, we often know the best way we learn, what we need to do to get the most out of a conversation, and what tricks we may have to engage in to retain information, i.e., mnemonic devices. These are all pieces of information that we incrementally learned about as we identified how we process information best over time. Researchers in this area would call this meta-cognition—thinking about how we think. Meta-cognition is an interesting concept and an important process for our children to learn about, think about, understand, and practice regularly. The more information and feedback we can give our children about how they learn to apply meaning to their world, the better.

Clarification skills go hand in hand with listening and processing. As we process information, we are thinking and evaluating the information. We think about what pieces we understood, what pieces we didn't understand, and what sense it all makes. We do this quickly as adults, but our children need to understand that to make a good, well thought-out decision, they must also have all the information. They need guidance with regard to what questions they need to ask, what information needs to be clarified, and what the possible outcomes may be. Without proper and complete information, poor decisions are frequent outcomes. By learning to ask open-ended questions sometimes and closed questions at other times, the goal is that our children will learn to ask good clarifying questions so that good decisions can be made. It is important for a child to understand that open ended questions open up discussion, and closed questions tend to get precise, yes or no answers and shut down further discussions. We should practice identifying and using these types of questions as a good learning experience for our children.

Problem solving is a complex task. It requires levels of understanding and the ability to ask good clarifying questions. It requires a child to process possible options and evaluate the outcomes of each. There is no magic about it. It takes time, experience, maturity, quality feedback and discussions about decisions and/ or situations. It doesn't come overnight for our developing children and yet they begin to problem solve from the moment they are born:

Hungry = cry.
Wet = cry.
Want a cookie = pull over a chair or pull out a drawer and climb up.
Need a calculator for class = borrow a friend's, beg mom for a new one, or baby-sit for money and buy a personal calculator.

Be presented with beer at a party at age fifteen = Say no, leave the party, call for a ride, or drink the beer.

Many options will often boil down to one final decision. The goal is that it be a good decision. Our children must learn to problem solve by taking in the information, processing it, evaluating the options, and making a decision. This is truly a difficult task, if time and energy are not devoted to it.

Self-advocacy skills are crucial. As adults, we need to express our needs and seek the necessary resources to accomplish a task or personal goal. If we can't do this, we spend a lot of time avoiding, procrastinating, or "spinning our wheels." Ultimately, without self-advocacy skills, an individual is often perceived as a voiceless victim or a convenient doormat. I truly believe, no parent has "victim" or "doormat" as a goal for their child, but at the same time I often wonder if parents realize that self-advocacy skills can start very early in life and can be nurtured and fostered every single day. We need to start our children's practice and feedback opportunities now, if it hasn't been started earlier.

As much as we want to fix all the problems in our children's lives, they need to struggle a bit and speak up for themselves. They need to figure out what to say and to whom in order to have their personal needs met. This is often very painful to watch as a parent; however, often we worry about it for a far greater portion of time than it takes for our children to either take care of the problem for themselves or just move on past it. Furthermore, we often project our own fears and insecurities on them without ever intending to do so. We must be very careful about this. There really is no reason that a basic "run of the mill" eleven-year old can't ask her teacher for help or her guidance counselor for some advice. There is no reason that an eight-year old can't ask the librarian to help find a book. These are tiny steps to developing self-advocacy skills our children will continue to call upon as they go through their life journey.

I repeat. The world can be a scary place. Without the necessary coping skills that we must nurture and encourage within our children, it can be even riskier and scarier. It is our ultimate role, as parents, to focus on these coping skills every chance we get. I'd rather see a child take a calculated step in using these skills early on so that he can experience the feeling of self-advocacy and learn from a situation rather than watch a parent do it for him over and over again. The message we send our children, although we would never state it, is, "I know you can't do it, so I will do it for you." By jumping in to solve problems before allowing a child to try to manage it, the parent will be creating a dependent adolescent who takes little responsibility for himself and believes his parents will bale him out every time.

Watching our children grow into fully capable, competent and confident young adults is an awesome experience. A culmination of hundreds of decisions we've made along the way results in a "grown up." As we allow our children to step into the "big scary world" we shouldn't hesitate to seek support and guidance from a trusted mentor or a trained professional. The school and community organizations can help address any concerns if, in fact, we believe our child may be dabbling in a risky behavior and may not have solid coping skills. We need to seek the support, advice, and help we may need. We will need all the strategies we can get, but we should keep in mind that coping skills don't happen over night. Practice and experience must be built into our children's lives, long before the adolescent years begin. (Big hint: When a child is two, four or six years old, parents should ask themselves, "Will it matter in ten years?)

Solid coping skills will strengthen our children's ability to handle the issues that are prevalent in our "big scary world." The issues must be open for discussion, and the guidelines we set must be enforced, but ultimately, it is our children who will make decisions that will either keep them safe or put them in potentially difficult or harmful situations.

There are hundreds of topics to discuss with our children. The reality is, however, once we think we've covered them all, there will be new scary things. The following ten topics are the ones I continuously keep in the forefront of my mind as a parent and professional. It should be a mandated law that parents talk to their children about each one of them—when the child is ready, not when the parent is ready. Even if it is uncomfortable, parents must put their child's needs first. Remember, the world out there is a complex and often confusing place. Our children are faced with these topics all the time. The following topics are not in any priority. These "hot topics" are equally important and parents should be on the lookout for all of them at simultaneous moments, and be ready to help their child when the child can't rely on their own developing skill set.

Drugs

I will never claim to be an expert on the drug situation in America or anywhere else in the world. However, I am a realist and an expert on adolescent behavior. I also know that as a parent we cannot afford to believe that our children will never face the offer of drugs. At one point or another, every adolescent will have the opportunity to drink alcohol or use an illegal substance before the age of twenty-one. Sadly enough, it will probably occur before they leave high school. Frequently, it may occur before they leave middle school.

Drugs come in a variety of shapes and types these days. We must stay abreast of what is out there. We can watch the news, jump on the Internet, and go to parent workshops or community discussions about helping children deal with the prevalence of drugs in our community. Our adolescents are bombarded with options and opinions regarding whether or not to get involved with drugs. The TV tells them one thing, their friends tell them something else. Our words say one thing, but perhaps our actions show them something else. We need to be aware of conflicting messages and talk to our children so they can begin to sort it all out.

Often it may be better to just listen to our children and their friends as they talk about what so-and-so (perhaps, one of the most popular kids in town) is up to. Attending open discussions, reading magazines and newspaper, talking with our own friends, and even "eavesdropping" can give us a big clue as to what the latest trend regarding drugs is for kids of our children's age group.

Trendy drugs among adolescents, including marijuana (weed or pot), crack, cocaine, ecstasy, heroine, steroids, alcohol and tobacco, are always changing, and we must keep abreast of the subject. A very scary reality is that adolescents are now using over-the-counter drugs such as Robitussin, Coriciden, and other cold medicines, or prescription drugs, such as Ritalin, at an alarming rate for the purpose of getting high. Parents should take a moment to "surf the net" regarding these trendy drug uses among adolescents. Although it is terrifying, it won't take long to find the information. If it is at our fingertips within minutes, it is probably at our computer savvy children's fingertips within seconds. These over-the-counter and/or prescription drugs are cheap, easily accessible, and their use can frequently go unnoticed. Parents should stay abreast of these trends among adolescents. It is possible that a parent's awareness could save his child's life.

The more we know, or are at least familiar with, the more likely our ears will perk up when we hear something we should be paying attention to. Parents need to stay alert and be confident in their ability to talk to their child about drugs. It may be vitally important to your child's life.

Ask yourself: *"Do I know everything I can about trendy and accessible drugs in my adolescent's world?"*

Sex

Sex has been around forever, but every kid thinks he/she invented it. We need to talk to other parents, stay connected, and talk to our children directly about sexual activity and what our expectations are, as well as some ways to get out of sexually uncomfortable situations. We need to listen to what our children are saying and asking us for. Our children may need help to problem solve. Friends may be giving mixed signals or sharing information that a child may not understand yet. They may need us to listen, clarify, or give guidance on the topic of sexual activity. It is a very confusing topic for many of our adolescents who are exposed by the various forms of media to so much information and sexual messages at such early ages.

Adolescent bodies change rapidly and dramatically. It takes time for their minds and emotions to catch up. The reality is that as an adolescent moves through their middle school years and high school years, hormonal changes and opportunities to have sexual experiences come together. The option to have sex or not, whether it is oral sex or intercourse, really is our children's choice. (There's a scary thought.) As uncomfortable as it may be for us, we must talk to our children long before the night before the prom. The reality is that prom night may be too late for many teenagers.

During early childhood development, a child must get clear messages from his parents about making choices that keep his/her body safe. At this age, more importantly a child needs the competence to weigh the consequences of his/her decisions around sex and the confidence to make the healthy decisions. A word of caution to all parents: Our sons can be daddies as easily as our daughters can be mommies. Some parents fall into the trap of believing only their girls need to protect their bodies. It's a "guy thing" as well.

Furthermore, sexually transmitted diseases have no preference for males or females. Both sexes are in equal danger of contracting sexual diseases they may have to deal with forever. We mustn't make the mistake of allowing or inadvertently encouraging a double standard. The decisions, choices, and consequences are a reality regardless of the sex of our children. We can help our children make good, well thought-out decisions early in childhood and throughout adolescence before the consequences of the poorly thought-out decisions automatically rule out some future choices for him or her.

Ask yourself: *"Do I understand that sexual activity is an option for my adolescent? Have I talked to my adolescent about the consequences of engaging in sexual activity during the adolescent years?"*

Dating

Dating is a natural way of learning to develop emotionally strong relationships. It is a time to test the skills that have been nurtured and developed, and a time to make decisions about what type of person someone wants to spend intimate time with. Dating allows for an opportunity to find out what type of person complements another's personal strengths and weaknesses. It is a necessary part of growing up. Our children will go through dating with highs and lows—good times and some tough times. Will he or she be ready for it?

Dating is a topic that is particular to each family. What are the rules about this? Does the child understand the expectations? What is the "norm" with this among the child's peers? Long before "dating age" a child should understand what the parents' expectations will be. If it is "normal" that a parent meets all friends before the child goes out, then it will seem natural for a child to invite his new friend over to introduce her to his parents.

We need to reach out to understand what "dating" means to our children. Is it going to the movies with groups of kids or a one-to-one relationship? At what point is it acceptable for the parent to allow and support this one-to-one relationship?

The whole notion of relationships must be explored thoroughly with a child before dating occurs. Parents are their children's primary example for relationships. They have an obligation to help their children process their relationship experiences as they occur. Every child will vary with regard to his or her ability to develop, monitor, and manage relationships. Once an adolescent has begun to date, parents need to be prepared to be supportive when a relationship breaks up or a date becomes abusive or too controlling. In the early stages of learning to develop dating relationships, break-ups are inevitable. Dysfunctional and/or unhealthy relationships may also arise in a child's dating experiences. Parents need to stay vigilant and be ready to help their child work through difficult relationships in order to develop appropriate and strong relationships.

Coping strategies are absolutely necessary when it comes to relationships and dating. This may be a very important time for us to reflect on our own coping skills when it comes to developing, maintaining, or managing relationships with the opposite sex. Our actions speak loudly to our children, and they will continue to observe and reflect on how we nurture our relationships. The norms we establish in our personal relationships are the ones our children will see on a regular basis. Our children learn from us all the time without exception. They watch our relationship exchanges for clues about how to handle their own relationships. Dating should provide for a lot of conversations with the emerging adult in our home. We should remember that we are the adults—the ones responsible for our children. We'll need to take the necessary steps to know their dates and understand where their relationships are going, as much as possible, without stifling their ability to learn from the "dating relationships."

Ask yourself: *"Does my adolescent have the maturity and necessary coping strategies to become involved in developing dating relationships?"*

Friends

Friends come in all sizes and shapes. Some are good influences and some are not. Some have been in our child's life forever, and some have not. Some of their parents we know, and some we don't. A critical concept here is to know as much about our child's friends as possible. If we don't know who the players are, supporting our children may be quite challenging. We need to listen to what our children say about their friends and try not to pass too much judgment. If our son starts feeling like we judge all of his friends, trust me, he will stop talking. We need to walk a fine line here. We should offer our home to our children and their friends as often as possible. We will learn a lot and be able to make sure they are as safe as possible at the same time.

The topic of friends naturally leads to the important topic of peer pressure. Most of us hang out with people like us, in our estimation. Our friends typically share similar interests, backgrounds, or goals. Guess what? This is true for children, too. Nothing makes me chuckle more than when a parent tells me that his kid is hanging out with "those kids" and "those kids" are no good. The funny part is when, sometimes only minutes later, a parent of one of "those kids" names the child of the first parent as being a bad influence on *her* child.

So, I am left wondering, which peer is the "bad peer" for the other? And, what is it that draws them to each other? Sometimes it's a common sport, a mutual friend, or the excitement of being associated with a "risk taker." Whatever it is, parents take note: The peer group of our children includes our children. The fact is that peer pressure can be a bad thing or a very good thing.

The belief that peer pressure is a bad thing can often be true. When our gut feeling tells us this, we must use great caution. Before passing judgment, we should stop and listen, observe and think, talk to our child, and be aware of the fact that all adolescents need a feeling of belonging. For some reason, our child has sought the peer group's acceptance, and the peer group has welcomed him in. What is it that draws and holds our child to this peer group? We must always pause and ask ourselves that question honestly.

However, the opposite type of peer pressure exists more frequently than people realize. I challenge parents to find examples in their child's life where the peer pressure is a good thing. Quite often, it is due to peer pressure that a child will run for a leadership position in school or stick with a team sport because all their friends are on it or be challenged to study harder because their friend has made a bet that they can out score them on an upcoming test. These are examples of positive peer pressure. We can use them to our advantage if we pay attention, accept the group as they are, and stay vigilant that the peer group is a healthy organization for our child to be a part of.

The same advice holds true with every type of peer pressure. Before passing judgment, we should stop and listen, observe and think, and talk to our child. When our child does become associated with a group of peers and "folds" to peer pressure, good or bad, we should try to understand what need the group serves for our child. If the group is one that associates itself with risky behaviors or socially unacceptable decisions, then it is our obligation to learn as much as possible about the members of his "peer group." We should talk to him about the pressures associated with his peers. Of course, it would be a dream (and highly unlikely) if a child could clearly articulate the reasons he enjoys being a part of this group.

From our perspective, we can share our observations and feelings about the members of his peer group, but we must do this fairly. We must stay alert to our own judgments and do so fairly so as not to shut down communication with our child. Our son or daughter "belongs" to the group we are judging and speaking of. One false move and his perception of our conversation may cause him to not hear what we feel the need to say. Carefully worded and objective observations shared honestly along with good open-ended questioning techniques can help keep the door to communication open.

Remember, above all else, our job as parents is to keep our children safe, and facilitate the development of solid coping skills. Peer pressure, whether we consider it good or bad, does allow for many opportunities to dialogue about relationships, behaviors, and decisions with our adolescent. These are not usually easy dialogues, but they are always important and necessary.

Ask yourself: *"Have I taken advantage of opportunities to get to know my adolescent's friends, and have I talked to my adolescent about his peer group?"*

Slipping grades

An adolescent's school grades may vary from time to time. None of us have probably given 100 percent of ourselves 100 percent of the time. It's rare that our daily work tasks are "graded" individually. Usually, in our professional world, it is our overall performance that we get feedback on. Our daily tasks are complied and evaluated by our supervisors over time, not usually daily. For our adolescent, their tasks are broken down and graded several times each day. Overall, we as parents need to look for consistency over time and patterns of performance. Fluctuations can occur and should be noted, but the overall picture is what is important in the end.

Grades may slip for no apparent reason. A tough test, a difficult chapter, an unprepared student, or a change in the teacher's expectations can all cause a grade change. Either way, if a grade slips, it should absolutely cause us to have a discussion with our child. Listen to what she says. Watch her body language, as well. Often the slipping grades are a first sign that something is going on, and the child may need our help to straighten it out.

We should continue to nurture the self-advocacy skills within our children by role playing various possibilities to boost their grades. However, if the problem is too overwhelming, it is important that we become more involved. We need to be there to support, but know that our child has to take steps to help himself or herself in the day-to-day responsibilities of school. There's no need to go crazy over this situation. If we think back, we probably did not always have consistent A's on our report cards either. We really need to talk to our children, listen to them, be able to make a decision to get involved, or make the decision to back off and let them learn to negotiate a tough situation through the use of self-advocacy skills and natural consequences. This may be very hard to do, but again, we need to think about the long-term goals versus the short-term objective. We, in consultation with our adolescent, have to be the decision-maker on this "slipping grade" situation. No two sets of parents will handle the slipping grade situation the same way, but it must be kept in perspective.

Obviously, during this decision-making time, we must know our child's typical patterns regarding grades and be aware of major changes. Slipping grades can often indicate an area of a child's life that may need some support. If things aren't becoming clearer regarding the slipping grades, we shouldn't hesitate to call the teacher or guidance counselor. There are several avenues of support we can access by contacting our child's guidance counselor or school psychologist.

Just keep it in perspective. One poor grade does not indicate that the world is ending. A pattern of slipping grades, however, may indicate that something is awry in your child's world. Stay vigilant and try as best you can to communicate with your child and help him explore ways that he can learn from the experience and plan ways to help himself in school. It is important to encourage him to use the self-advocacy skills you have been teaching him to seek support systems within the school if necessary.

Ask yourself: *"Why are my adolescent's grades slipping, and, if necessary, have I called the right people to get help?"*

Inappropriate "overheard" conversations

When we "overhear" a conversation between our adolescent and her friends that seems "inappropriate," something is probably up. Adolescence is a time in a child's life where friends of equally limited experience will try to help each other through a variety of situations. This is not an awful thing, and can sometimes actually be helpful. However, because coping skills develop at varying rates, based on life experiences, and because adolescence is a time of general confusion, we may overhear conversations that may sound illogical or twisted. We shouldn't pass these conversations off as irrelevant but, on the other hand, we shouldn't always leap into action either. We need to weigh the facts and talk to our children. We should trust our gut feeling on this and talk to our child so that she knows we are concerned about her safety and/or the safety of her friends. Now is probably not the time for big lectures, but supportive conversations are a must.

Talking is good, but more important is listening. We need to be sure we heard what we thought we heard before we go ahead and pass judgment. Once we have clarified that what we heard is what was actually said, we have some decisions to make. We need to let our children know that if someone's health and/or safety are at risk, the right thing to do is take action that will keep that person safe. If we have been talking to them about love and safety since they were little, they will already know. What the actual action is will depend on many factors: the context, the seriousness, the legalities, the friend's parents' knowledge of the situation, and our comfort level with the content. This is a life lesson for our child. He will learn that we will always want to know of his safety and thus, we must take action for someone else's child's safety as well.

Again, "overhearing" will lead to very important and necessary conversations that we must have. As uncomfortable as it may be, and our children may accuse us of "eavesdropping", we must follow up to be sure we heard what we thought we heard, and then take appropriate and necessary actions. Back to an already stated concept: We are the number one role model for developing relationships, problem solving, and implementing communication skills for our adolescents. We need to deal with the "overheard" conversations especially when they could be vitally important.

Ask yourself: *"Did I really hear that? And now what do I do with that information?"*

The School Dance Rules

My standard line, when my daughters and their friends began going to the middle school dances, was "No smoking, no drinking, no bumping, no grinding, and no kissing on the dance floor." Of course, I'd say it with a smile and a kiss on the forehead of each kid, regardless of whether or not I owned them, before they left my house to go to the dance. Because we lived only two houses away from the middle school, my house was often the gathering point. Now my girls recite the rules to me with a smile and a kiss. Although the statement is somewhat ridiculous, at least they know that I will be thinking about what they are doing while they are at the dance. They also know what my expectations are for their behaviors, even when they are not in my presence. That is my goal.

When our babies were little, we knew everything and could be with them every minute if we chose to. We were able to control their world, sign them up for activities we chose, and select which children would be allowed to play with our little precious ones. Now, as they begin to widen their circle of friends and pick their own activities, our amount of control is decreasing. But our children always need to know that we continue to keep them in our mind, even when they are not home. By having little rituals or teasing phrases that have been repeated again and again, perhaps a hope is that our voice will stay in their heads. There will be those times, like it or not, that as we watch our children and their friends go out our door, we'll have to cross our fingers and start praying hard.

Clear expectations, a sense of humor, and love will get a parent through a lot of the times when she can't be with her children. And there will be many of these times throughout their adolescent years.

Ask yourself: *"Does my adolescent understand my expectations even when he is not in my presence?"*

Our Child's Commitment to Bigger Things

Commitments can come and go, but it is important for our adolescents to understand that their word is one thing that people will learn to trust or not trust depending on the experiences and interactions they have with those around them. When a commitment is made, it is similar to a promise. Follow through is a must. Commitments relate directly back to Step 7. Promises are made to parents, siblings, employers, the church, and God. Commitments and promises are bigger than our children and each must be treated respectfully. The more times our children can see the correlation between making commitments and having faith in a promise, the more likely the invisible commitments, such as keeping promises, following their own words, or following expectations set for them, will remain as a high priority to their conscience. Commitments are serious things, and once made should be handled with care, always. We should model follow-through on our own commitments so that it becomes the norm and thereby feels "right" for our children. We are their number one role model.

A commitment to others shows respect and kindness to others. If kindness is fostered, nurtured, and expected, a commitment to kindness toward others emerges and becomes a consistent habit of how a child relates socially to the world around him. Kindness is a golden rule. Kindness really does matter. Everybody has the right to live in the community they have chosen, and we all have an obligation as a neighbor and a citizen to allow the same rights we want to be granted to our neighbors. We all, including our children, need to acknowledge this and take responsibility for caring for those around us. It is the only way we can make the world a kinder place. This also places the responsibility to model kindness on us, the parents.

The notion that kindness matters and is the right thing to do as a citizen or neighbor must be encouraged early on. Community volunteers are always wanted. The local nursing home, church group, or an elderly neighbor could always use help. Babysitting, caring for a neighbor's dog or helping a teacher after school are all common ways that children learn early on how to help others. As parents we should also model service and commitment to others. Our children are always comparing our words to our actions. When we serve others, our commitment to kindness can be seen by our children through our observable behaviors. This is important. As they mature into adolescence, this normal pattern of helping others will hopefully be ingrained in them and it will feel comfortable and natural for them to look for ways to reach out and help others around them. Thus, this kindness shown to others is a perfect setup for demonstrating a commitment to the world or concepts that are greater than ourselves. An interesting notion that I believe in is that a commitment to respect and kindness may actually, in time, help make the world a bit less scary.

Ask yourself: *"Have I instilled a commitment of respect for others in my adolescent?"*

Language in Music and on TV

Adolescents are going to watch TV, MTV, and listen to music with inappropriate language embedded into it all. Even sitcoms, which used to be "family shows," now incorporate questionable language and themes on a daily basis. Shows that used to be aired at 9:00 p.m. are now syndicated and on TV at 4:00 p.m. Gone are the days of *The Brady Bunch, The Partridge Family,* and *The Waltons.*

It is important we talk to our children about this and know that the behaviors and messages that are prevalent on TV and in music are often in direct conflict with our family values. Our children need to continuously be reminded that these behaviors and words they see and hear around them are not what we expect at home or in the community. Most kids understand this, but reminders are always helpful. The more frequently they see these behaviors and attitudes in the bombardment of various media, the more acceptable it may seem to them. They need the adults around them to help process and sort out this conflicting information.

I am a proponent of speaking up when I see something on MTV, TV, or hear it on the radio that, to me, is inappropriate. I may not be able to change the laws about what's allowed to be aired, but at least my children know my expectations of what I think about behaviors, styles, and language they are bombarded with by the world. All parents have that very same option. We need to speak up, talk to ourselves, and think out loud. It is hard to teach modesty when the outfits our children see and the language they hear regularly are so provocative. These conflicting messages, however, provide us with hundreds of conversations we can have with our adolescents if we choose to have them. On a humorous note, I believe my children are sick of hearing me say this particular phrase whenever inappropriate clothing is on MTV, an award show, a sitcom, or in public: "I hope she only paid half price for that outfit since she's only wearing half an outfit." Or, when it comes to language: "I hope he doesn't kiss his mother with that mouth."

Yes, my daughters roll their eyes, but now at ages fourteen and fifteen, they will say these very same statements to me before I even get my own statements out. If nothing else, they know my expectations of appropriate dress and language. By providing thoughts and expectations, the hope is that it gives them a guide to use in this confusing world they must live in.

Ask yourself: "Does my adolescent have a clear understanding of what my expectations are for how she presents herself to the world through her choice of language and dress?"

Pros and Cons of Organized Sports

I was one of the first girls allowed to play in the community baseball league in my town when I was growing up. I'm not positive, but my sister could have been the only other girl. That was quite an experience. Basically, the boys played baseball and I checked out my split ends out in the outfield as my father yelled from the bleachers, "Debi, pay attention!"

Organized sports have come a long way since 1976, and I am a believer in them for many reasons. But I also offer a word of caution about them. Some may take objection with organized sports being in the "Big Scary World" category, but as with peer pressure, it can have positives and negatives connected to it. The positives are obvious—a sense of belonging, experience on a team, building relationships, building confidence, building self esteem, experience with commitment, and fun are all examples. The other side is really just a concern to be raised about the amount of pressure organized sports can place on an adolescent. Perhaps it's not even that scary, but it is something to be considered.

The amount of pressure is the key. Pressure comes in a variety of forms. There is pressure to perform and pressure from their peers. There is pressure to compete and succeed and pressure to try out for the "travel team." There is pressure to "get out on that field and crush 'em," even when they don't want to or are afraid to disappoint someone. Sometimes there is pressure to do things with or for the team that may be risky. We all watch the news and have heard the stories of poor decisions like hazing or team initiation rituals being made by "several members of the team." Often individually, each kid is a wholesome model student. So we must acknowledge that sometimes, just sometimes, team peer pressure can be associated with pressures that manipulate our adolescents into making a bad decision.

The other piece to organized sports is a piece of a bigger issue. Over-programming our adolescents puts time pressures on them and then they don't know how to occupy down time constructively. Our adolescents are often so programmed that when they have available time, there's been no opportunity to develop hobbies and interests that are completely and independently generated. The world offers our children opportunities that are timely, fun, and full of instant gratifica-tion. The lack of control in their over-programmed world may cause them to seek poor and/or intense opportunities that may lead to out-of-control behaviors, i.e., binge drinking, experimenting with drugs, folding to peer pressure, or just acting upon a very bad idea for the sheer excitement of it.

For me, the bottom line is that there are numerous wonderful aspects of a child's participation in organized sports that have been written about in articles and books in probably every conceivable language. But, as a parent, balance and vigilance is the key. Too much of a good thing is sometimes something to watch out for. The big scary world is a tricky one. We need to be vigilant. We need to watch closely, talk to our children, and be sure they are making the decisions about how they manage their organized sports and activities. They may need our help, but *they* should be controlling it, not us. We should ask questions, and make sure they are living their own dreams, when it comes to sports. We shouldn't be living *our* dreams through *their* sports.

Ask yourself: *"Have I given my adolescent a healthy balance of experiences so that he can learn to control his own participation in life?"*

If we really sit back and brainstorm everything that our adolescents are facing, as they become independent citizens of the world, we may become overwhelmed. However, regardless of the scary thoughts and all the fears we may have as our children take bigger steps into the world, the goal basically stays the same. The goal is to take in all the information we can, filter it as best we can and then make our parenting decision align with our desire to raise a healthy adult. We should always try our best to keep them safe, even when we know we have to allow them to grow.

Some kids are natural risk-takers. Others just need a little coaxing from the world around them. By paying attention, which is a full time job as a parent, we may be able to influence the amount of risk facing our children. It is true though that we all needed to take a certain amount of risk to grow and learn and have fun; however, too much risk is the dangerous key point here. Trying to minimize the consequences of the necessary risk-taking, while watching our children grow is a fascinating balancing act.

A real tempting choice we have is to take every precaution to keep our chil-dren safe, but the reality is, we will not always be with them at every minute, nor would that be appropriate. But let's say it was possible. There would still be no guarantee that our children would be forever protected from harm. Things hap-pen. That's life. We can, however, do everything within our power, but some-times we just have to cross our fingers and pray hard. That's the real truth about letting our children grow into healthy adults.

As the school principal, I greet my students at the curb every morning as they get out of their parents' cars. I welled up with tears, one day, when I realized that every day, without fail, one mother closed her eyes for just a split second as she blessed herself while her eighth-grade daughter stepped from the car, said good-bye, and closed the car door. In that second of a silent prayer, there was an overt sign of the hope and love she has for her daughter, and every fear she has for her daughter in the big scary world probably flashes through her mind. The message to her daughter, however, was a very powerful one: "I love you and I pray God protects you till I see you again." I don't doubt for a second that this mom repeats this ritual each time her daughter leaves her house. What an incredible lesson for me when I put those little pieces together.

We can't, nor do we really want to eliminate every risk our children will ever have to endure. However, whenever possible, we must remain vigilant of these risks, try to minimize some, and convey that we are always thinking of our chil-dren when they are out there facing the world alone. The power of positive think-ing (and prayer, I believe) is a powerful thing. It's free, always available, and within our control. We, as parents, might as well use it since so many things are out of our control.

The bottom line is, so many of these facets of the big scary world all boil down to consequences of being involved in potentially risky behaviors. And guess what? It started when they were two—a good ten years ago. Did we ask ourselves back then, "Will it matter in ten years?" Everything matters now that we're living with an adolescent. We'll just have to hang in there keeping our eyes open and our ears tuned in, and our mind alert. We need to try our best to help our child under-stand The Big Scary World around him, so it won't seem so big and scary.

Keeping in mind that everything does matter in our adolescents' world, it is important to reflect on the Big Scary World and get a sense of how well we, and our adolescents, are managing it. Here are the reflection questions already pre-sented in the previous paragraphs. They are here again as a quick reference. Check in on yourself from time to time.

Ask yourself:

1. *"Do I know everything I can about trendy and accessible drugs in my adolescent's world?"*

2. *"Do I understand that sexual activity is an option for my adolescent? Have I talked to my adolescent about the consequences of engaging in sexual activity during the adolescent years?"*

3. *"Does my adolescent have the maturity and necessary coping strategies to become involved in developing dating relationships?"*

4. *"Have I taken advantage of opportunities to get to know my adolescent's friends and have I talked to my adolescent about his peer group?"*

5. *"Why are my adolescent's grades slipping and, if necessary, have I called the right people to get help?"*

6. *"Did I really hear that? And now what do I do with that information?"*

7. *"Does my adolescent understand my expectations even when he is not in my presence?"*

8. *"Have I instilled a commitment of respect for others in my adolescent?"*

9. *"Does my adolescent have a clear understanding of what my expectations are for how she presents herself to the world through her choice of language and dress?"*

10. *"Have I given my adolescent a healthy balance of experiences so that he can learn to control his own participation in life?*

Part V:

It's Just An Illusion:
Making the Working-Mom
Thing Look Easy

Unless a woman is a magician, the "easy working mom" thing is an illusion. It's never really "easy." So the question comes back around that people often ask me: "How do you do it?"

The reality is, not many of us are working full time while raising our family because it is just "so enjoyable." At times, it is the furthest thing from being described as fulfilling. The truth is we work to pay the bills and the money and benefits only come to us if we go to work. I do believe that the ultimate fantasy for most working moms starts with "Hit the Powerball numbers." The truth is very few of us actually hit the Powerball numbers, so somehow millions of women around the world have figured out how to do this thing called "The Working Mom Thing." Some moms find it easier to do than others do on a regular basis, and everyone of us has good days and bad. However, that being said, there are routines, and adjustments we can make to better our chances of having some sense of calm in our crazy hectic days.

The following suggestions are just those—suggestions. They are not guarantees, nor are they recommendations. I would never assume that what works for me to keep my life a bit more stable is a must for anyone else. That would be ridiculous. With that said, however, I certainly welcome the opportunity to share some simple strategies that have simplified my life. They have allowed me to organize myself in a way that helps to calm my nerves from time to time. In all honestly, these ideas help tremendously, but life happens. And when life does feel out of control, melt-downs happen. Usually a good cry will clear the mind so that the soul and heart can get back on track. The "Working Mom Thing" is never simple. Moms should not fool themselves into believing it is.

These twenty-five suggestions come in no specific order. They didn't come to me in any order either. They just seemed to emerge. Read them, reflect on them, use some, and feel free to dismiss some. Whatever works for you will be the key to providing the illusion that this working mom thing can be done easily—with some planning and some "magic tricks."

1. Color-code your kids.

I know this sounds crazy, but have each of your children pick a color during the summer and then get the backpack, folders, binder, and lunchbox to match that color. This can make life a little easier. Rather than yelling every morning or evening, "Whose binder is this?" it is more fun to yell "Who's purple?" You've got to have a little fun whenever you can even if it includes sounding a bit ridiculous.

2. Folders empty out on the kitchen table right after school.

Train your child from an early age to take out all school notices as he enters the house after school. Have him put them on the kitchen table. Then, that evening, sift through this unending pile of school papers as quickly as possible. Sign permission slips immediately, and put the rest in a different pile to be looked at later, if it is important enough to do so. You may have to make some quick decisions. Some stuff seems important, so put it in the pile. Some of this stuff won't matter if you wait long enough. If it's garbage initially, just throw it away. If you put it in the pile and it really is just garbage, it will still be garbage when you finally find the time to look at it.

3. Go through the junk on your counter every weekend.

I know that sounds harsh, but it usually is just junk. This is a necessary task that takes a few minutes or else your counters will become inundated with stuff and unmanageable by any human being. Maybe in front of the TV, during your favorite show or while making a shopping list for yourself or husband, would be a good time for you to sort through this pile. This is the kind of routine that doesn't need to happen daily. But at some point, it must happen. As stated above, some stuff doesn't matter if you wait long enough. So now maybe what you thought may be important information a week ago is now just garbage. Throw it out. A variation of this technique is to go through the daily mail while standing at the garbage can. Other than the bills, most of what comes through your mailbox is junk. Challenge yourself to throw it out immediately. Don't even be tempted to put it in your pile on the counter. You really won't miss it! Just throw it out!

4. Everything goes on one calendar.

Often I have noticed that the most disorganized people have a calendar at home, one in their bag, and maybe an electronic organizer. Each tool has different information, which just confuses the heck out of a naturally disorganized person and their family. If you are one of these people, you need to *get it together!* This is key. Everything must go on one calendar. My faculty meetings, my husband's bowling and baseball schedules, parties for kids' friends, schedules for altar serving, and when to make brownies for whose class party are all on the calendar. Everything is on one calendar. And everyone can learn that this is the *master* family guide.

The next step, which will sound obvious, but must be said, would be to *look at it* daily to figure out the plan for the next couple of days. Overlaps will happen, and favors of friends will have to be asked, but you don't want to do that at the last minute. Having that one central family calendar will help you plan ahead and make life a bit smoother, especially during potentially stressful times.

I have a friend who goes one step further. Once she has put something on the calendar, she color-codes each of her family members with a specific highlighter color. Then, in a glance, she can see if a particular family member needs to be somewhere on any given day. This is a bit over the top for me, but it is the ultimate in family organization.

5. Keep tape by the calendar.

My calendar is ugly. I make no apologies for it. There are schedules all over it and fliers hanging from it. Every school flier or invitation is taped up until the event happens and then it is promptly ripped down. This sounds like a simple, and perhaps ridiculous, suggestion; however, it has saved my life. An invitation comes in; I tape it up. A kid's club or activity is beginning; I tape up the whole flier, not just the information on it. A special announcement of some type comes in the mail; I tape that up. The calendar looks messy, but I have all the necessary details at my fingertips. Believe it or not, having the tape right near the calendar simplified my world. No more searching. Just grab the tape, which is right there on the counter, and tape the notice up. No one needs an expert to make this suggestion, and yet millions of us search for the tape dispenser for hours because we know we stuck it in a drawer somewhere. But, which drawer? Be proud of your tape. Leave it out in the open; right next to your messy calendar.

6. Have your kids list their friends and put their phone numbers right by the phone.

Each friend, first and last name, must be put on the list with a phone number. This makes life so much easier. It is unreasonable to believe that each of us could rattle off all of our children's friends' names at a moment's notice. It is hard enough to keep track of whose friend is whose, and we often don't know the last name of the friends talked about at home. Once you have your children make this list, tape it up. Tape it right up by the main phone. Enough said.

7. Sign up and make brownies for everything.

The occasion doesn't matter, the age of the kid doesn't matter, every hostess accepts them lovingly, every kid will eat them, and you don't get confused with which kid signed up to bring what. Everybody accepts brownies lovingly! I'll admit it. I tried to be creative once. I signed up to send in Halloween cups for the party. What a last minute pain in the neck and an ultimate disaster. No store has them at 11 o'clock at night, which is when I remembered them. Needless to say, my kid took leftover Christmas cups that I had in the pantry for the Halloween party. It was a pretty funny story, and a very practical lesson.

So now I make brownies for everything. It's a whole lot less stressful than running all over town looking for something you never had time to go get in the first place. My kids now tell their teachers, "My mom only makes brownies." It is a very liberating feeling. The brownies are my preference. Yours can be whatever you want. But the key is to keep a stock of it in your pantry and then sign up for it every chance you get.

8. Buy big packs and split them up for special gifts.

Twelve ornaments in one package at a large discount store equals twelve teacher gifts for under $15. Buy two sets and now you have very cute hostess gifts for the parties throughout the holidays as well. Just keep a few in your closet for the unexpected friend who pops in with a small gift, and you want to reciprocate. You've got them on hand if you have purchased the treats in bulk. If you keep a few wrapped in your closet, you'll look like you've thought of everything without being caught off guard.

9. Chocolate goes a long way.

Glass candy dishes from gift shops, Goodwill, or any other store along with some candies from a local grocery store make a perfect gift in a moment's notice. Keep a few of these types of things handy and you can whip up a teacher's gift, a hostess gift, or a surprise guest gift anytime. It is relatively inexpensive, and you can wrap it up nicely with some tissue paper that you should always have on hand, along with a set of blank note cards for a quick note to go with the gift.

10. Keep a list of "Ongoing Projects" nearby to do while watching TV.

Labeling photos, working on a craft project, organizing your kids' old school papers to put into a scrap book are just a few of those "ongoing projects." The bottom line is that as a parent we tend to want to get things in order as a way of preserving our children's childhood. I work with a running list of them in my mind. It may sound kind of sick, but it is true. I often think, in case I die I want my kids to have the information I have kept on them. This may sound strange, but it is true and a good motivator to get me moving on all my projects. If I am not here next year, next week, or when the kids are twenty-five and start asking questions, at least their personal histories are organized for each of them.

In keeping with the old adage, "Idle hands are the devil's workshop," idle hands are also wasted time. If you can multitask, you have a built-in advantage. By keeping these projects on hand, a few minutes here or there can become a valuable resource. Furthermore, the sense of accomplishment when a project is completed is extremely satisfying. When asked, "Where do you find the time to get those pictures in albums or scrapbooks put together?" Your honest response can be "Oh, here and there." The reality is we all have the same number of hours in a day, but how we use them can make a huge difference.

11. Never watch the TV only.

Do something! This is directly linked to the previous suggestion. TV is a huge time waster. The time goes by and there is nothing you can do to get that precious hour back. But if you "kill two birds with one stone," then you can make that hour productive. In front of the TV, I have made many Raggedy Ann dolls and knitted stockings for my fifteen nieces and nephews and my own four children. I've put labels on photos and then put them into the albums. I've written thank-you notes (*yes*, they still are very important), and gone through the piles of stuff from my kitchen counter, while watching a sitcom. Whatever you can do, while appearing to relax in front of the TV, is a productive use of time. One thing done is one less thing to have to get done from your never ending "To Do" list.

12. Keep individual photo albums for your kids.

I started creating individual photo albums for each of my children when my first child was born, and now I see what a benefit there is to it. I always get the free second set of prints when I develop a roll of film: one for me and one for the kids' albums.

For my family, I always have five albums going at all times: mine plus one each for the kids. At times it seems overwhelming, but what I have learned is that through this organizational strategy, when one of my children needs a "baby picture" for school or she has to make a "timeline" of her life, it is very easy to pull out her own albums and the task is at my fingertips. In addition to this, their childhood is ready for reminiscing. Older family members, who have passed on, are always there when the kids thumb through their own albums. Mine is the "master set of all pictures," but each child's photo album primarily focuses on his or her own childhood. I have made an effort, though, to be sure important family members (grandparents, aunts, uncles, cousins) are embedded somewhere in each of their albums.

A timeline I work off of includes updating the photo albums twice a year; summer and Christmas break. By doing this, I find that I can keep the number of photos to be put into the albums manageable so that I don't end up feeling so overwhelmed that I put off the whole task.

13. Start a pillow book.

Pillow books are a wonderful way to talk to your children and keep a journal of their lives at the same time. When my oldest child was turning eleven years old, I began the ritual of a pillow book. This is a journal that goes back and forth between my daughter and me. We write about our day or ask each other questions and then slip it under each other's pillow at night. It goes back and forth and is never discussed in the "light of day." It has been a wonderful experience, and I now do it with all my children. I have to admit, the pillow books have been far more successful with my daughters than with my sons. It could be that the girls are older and I was more diligent when it started or that my girls are just more expressive than my boys. You may find similar, or very different, results with your own children.

What started out as a nightly thing has changed to a weekly or monthly surprise under their pillows. It has served as a wonderful tool for sharing our thoughts with each other. An unexpected bonus of the pillow books is the fact that it captures the kids' thinking at that time. It is a forever keepsake of the little ones' concerns, fears, and funny moments. It is far more fun than just a diary or journal. We can look back on it and the memories that have been shared within it. As part of the written exchange I have also been able to ask about events, ideas, and situations so that they are forever documented in their personal pillow books.

14. Get someone else to do the shopping and laundry.

Not everyone is fortunate enough to live with a saint, but most husbands or other family members will step up and help out if asked. But beware. If you ask your spouse or child to do the shopping, just know that it won't be done exactly the way you want, but it will be done, so shut up! This may be the hard part. You will, however, have to be willing to go shopping on occasion to stock up on special supplies unless you get really good at thinking about everything you may ever need and remember to add it to the list. Be as specific as you can be, but accept what you get. One person I know photocopies a standard list of staples that are used regularly. Each week the list is taped to the refrigerator, and she circles the items she runs out of during the week. In addition, she adds items as she thinks of them throughout the week. By the weekend, her list of needed groceries is complete.

Laundry is something else for which you can ask for support. A husband or a teenage child is just as capable as you are for doing the laundry. I have to be honest. In my case, almost everyone in my house is far more capable of doing the laundry than I am. All disastrous loads have been due to my hands.

A word of caution should you try out this suggestion: If you critique your husband each time he picks up the wrong type of milk, he will eventually say, "Then you do it." You just lost your greatest resource. Be careful. If you critique your adolescent every time he/she messes up the laundry and then step in to fix it, guess what? I bet that kid will continue to not understand how to do it. Guess who will continue to do all the laundry? Don't be a control freak. Give it up. Both the laundry and the grocery shopping can be done by someone else. Maybe not your way, but it can be done.

15. Who cares if the socks match?

Here's a revelation. Buy white socks only! Accept the fact that matching socks is a useless task. For myself, I only buy black or white socks. For the kids, I only buy white athletic socks or white footie socks. It doesn't really matter then for my two girls and two boys whose socks belong to who, as long as there are two socks per kid on any given day. I totally threw in the towel on this useless match-the-socks-game. I now keep a laundry basket of just socks in my room. It is a community pile. Everyone just digs right in and finds a pair of socks when they need to. I won't win the Mother of the Year Award with this home management strategy, but it has truly simplified my life. The dreaded matching-the-socks-game was the part I hated most about folding clothes. This dread would lead me to not fold any of the clothes. So now with a new attitude on non-matching socks, I have a lighter heart regarding the never-ending pile of laundry to fold.

16. Use the crock pot.

What a treasure! Load up the crock pot the night before and let it cook overnight. By the time you wake up, dinner for the day is done and you don't have to leave it cooking all day while you are at work. Or set it up the night before (which is a fancy way of saying, "dump all the stuff in"), leave it in the fridge overnight, take it out in the morning and plug it in before you leave for work. Let it cook all day, if that doesn't make you nervous. Either way you will have a lovely chicken, pork, beef, or soup dinner waiting for you and your family when the evening comes. There are hundreds of cook books on the market specifically designed for use with a crock pot. Find one you like or experiment with a favorite family recipe. Once you begin using your crock pot on a regular basis, the burden of "What's for dinner?" will become lighter. Remember, you, too, can look like a hero mom, if you really use that crock pot.

17. Freezer and extra fridge.

Every working woman can benefit from having an extra refrigerator and/or freezer in the basement. Look for a hand-me-down from someone who is moving, or treat yourself when the stores are having a great sale. For so many of us, the freezer and/or extra refrigerator is not a frivolous extra. These appliances are essentials for stabilizing our ability to manage our crazy working lifestyles. If you have a freezer and/or fridge stocked with staples for any meal, you can throw together a few *hors d'evours* for that impromptu "happy hour" on a Friday, or dig deep for a meal to throw into the crock pot on a cold winter day. Yes, you will probably spend more money on food because now you have the room to store it. However, in the long-run by having things handy in the spare freezer you will be less likely to have to buy meats at the high prices or treat your family to a fast food restaurant on a regular basis. Now you can buy in bulk or when the meat is on sale and stay stocked up.

18. Keep quick breads always handy.

Quick bread mixes such as banana bread, cranberry bread, or cinnamon swirl should always be kept handy. Throw in some nuts—go wild! Whether it is the next door neighbor's crisis, a new friend, a "forgotten about" party at work, or whatever, it doesn't matter. As long as you have a few of these quick breads handy, you can look like a hero in about an hour. They are delicious, always welcomed, and reduces the stress and cost of having to run to the store at the last minute.

19. Keep frozen (or canned) veggies, broth, and canned tomatoes in stock all the time.

If you have any pantry space at all, these three items hide a multitude of sins and can turn any leftover into a gourmet meal. They are great for the quick crock pot meal or easy soup. Keep them handy. You'll be able to whip up almost anything from these few simple ingredients to create family recipes. Play with various combinations. Be creative and have fun. Hey, it's a meal!

20. Subdivide big supplies of cheese and butter, and then freeze them.

I am convinced that if you throw cheese over anything, it will taste better. That is probably the theory that has earned me the title of "Lifetime Weight-Watcher," but nevertheless, it is true. Mozzarella freezes fine and melts fairly quickly. Cheese can help to spruce up anything quickly. Another must is butter. I hate running out of butter, so over time I have learned to keep an extra pound or two in the freezer. I haven't run out of butter in years doing this. It defrosts easily on the counter or in the refrigerator. I just replenish the stock regularly. It's always on the running, regular shopping list. And when these staple items are on sale, I really stock up. The wholesale stores sell cheese and butter in jumbo doses. This is the perfect time to subdivide it into freezer bags and always have both on hand.

21. Find fun friends.

This sounds like a cop-out, but it feels so good to be able to call a fun friend and say, "Either I have to go or else everyone else in my house has to go!" If it is a really fun friend, she will understand that feeling and say, "Let's go to the movies, or out for tea or a cocktail."

This time is critical, necessary, and often a life-saver. Friends who are pessimistic just become overwhelming. But friends who see the humor in life, fill you with laughter, share a tear or two, and tell you that you are normal and you can do this, are invaluable for your sanity as a working mom. They have faith in you, even if you are sucking wind in the "working mother" role at that time. I actually met some of my closest friends at the PTO meetings, but I really got to know them in the bottles of wine, cheese and crackers, and cups of tea that followed the PTO meetings. I believe there isn't a working woman out there who could survive without a few fun friends. Look for them. Seek them out. You will need them!

22. Believe it or not—make time for the PTO meetings.

When you make time for the PTO meetings at your child's school, it gives the illusion that you have time for your child's education. You network with women you never would meet because you don't do the drop-offs and pick-ups at the school yard gate. By attending the PTO meetings, you also get a quick "down and dirty" run down of who's who at the school and what is going on. For the one night a month, it is time well spent. You need to know about your child's day and his education. This is an easy way to get that information.

Availability for these PTO meetings can sometimes be tough, but here's an idea I stumbled upon that completely served my needs. When my children were little, and my husband Vinnie bowled on Thursday nights, I'd get upset because I couldn't go to all the meetings at my children's elementary school, because they were always held on a Thursday, which conflicted with bowling. Then I got smart. I made a deal with a great seventeen-year old. The deal was, during the school year she'd book every Thursday night for me for babysitting. If I used her, I paid her the fair price. If I didn't use her, I'd give her ten dollars for keeping herself available for me. I think in the three years we had this agreement, I didn't use her approximately five Thursdays. It was a brilliant move. I was able to go to important meetings, Christmas shopping, to Barnes and Nobles for peace and quiet, or out for dinner with my friends. My Thursday-night babysitter was a Godsend. Sometimes what seems extravagant to some extent is actually just what you need to keep your sanity and to keep informed. Both are very important when you are a working mom.

In addition, when you seek creative ways to find the time, and make yourself available to attend these meetings, you're likely to meet a few fun friends there who can relate to your world. Look for them. Seek them out. They are there and you will need them.

23. Keep a book, magazine, or blank note cards in the car at all times.

For those ten minutes before a drop-off of one kid and a pick-up of another, you need to keep that book handy. It may take you all season to read it, but it will be time well spent. All you may need is ten minutes to relax with a magazine you ordered but never had time to sit down to look at. For you true multi-taskers, by keeping a box of blank note cards in the car, you can jot a quick note or birthday wish to a friend. Your friend might just need that little friendly note from you to help get her through her day. We should always try to find time to be a good friend. This tidbit of advice goes right back to keeping up with those "ongoing projects." When you have ten minutes, and you accomplish something you perceive as productive, it feels good. Go ahead. *Do* it and then cross it off your list. If the book, the magazine, and/or the note cards are handy in your car, there's a good chance when you find yourself with ten free minutes that you'll accomplish one of those "little" tasks.

24. Books on tape while walking.

This is the ultimate multi-task maneuver. Very few of us have the luxury of time to sit each day and read from that fabulous novel everyone is talking about. We all are very busy. However, you can keep up to date with that "best seller" everyone is talking about at work if you fit it into the walk you are dying to take just to walk off the stress of a full day. Listening to a kind gentle voice tell you a story, while you are walking and trying to ignore the world around you, is a great stress reducer. A huge benefit is that you can partake in conversations going on in the cafeteria at work or with other mothers who did find time to read that book. You can stay current with the best-sellers and feel good about being a part of conversations. In the meantime, you have stayed physically active, too.

25. Drink your tea black!

I know this sounds stupid. However, the day I switched from milk and Sweet and Low to black tea was a revelation. I no longer needed to dig through my cabinet or ask for a Sweet and Low at the restaurant, use a spoon and then have garbage to throw away. I no longer needed to take that extra minute to go to the fridge, uncap the milk, pour two drops, recap the mild and replace it into the fridge and then stir again. Now I pour and go. It is so much easier. The other added bonus was a reduction of a few calories per cup (times several cups per day) and the true taste of a great hot cup of tea. Try it. You may actually like it!

What Kind of Kid Do You Want in Ten Years? The Choice Really is Yours!

So there you have it. The million decisions, reactions, and responses you make will result in a great adult. Hopefully, that is. It is impossible to predict the end result because there are so many uncontrolled factors involved, but what you choose to do when you answer the question "Will it matter in ten years?" may tip the scales in a direction that will lead to a productive, respectful, good citizen. If you've gotten through to this point in the book, you can see my passion. I believe we, as parents are capable of and must commit to raising the best possible citizens we can. This is hard work. Raising brats is easy.

The rewards of raising a great kid are immeasurable. There's nothing like it. Millions of people do it every day. Each of us can be included in those millions. Millions of people also raise brats who may have difficulty coping with what life throws at them as well. Each of us can be included in with those millions, too, if we so choose. The choice really is ours. And it doesn't start when the kid is twenty or fifteen or ten or eight, or even five years old. It starts at the earliest age possible. It definitely starts by age two when our children are already learning to interact and manipulate their world. By age two, our children will know what buttons to push and how to get us to fold. They will try everything to control their environment. So, will our decisions and statements matter when our children are two years old? Absolutely! Even when we're too busy to pay attention to our parenting decisions, for our children's sake, we must always pay attention. The decisions we make will continue to matter throughout our children's lives.

As our children aim toward independence, risks will be taken. Calculated risks on our part, hopefully, and stupid risks on their part, probably. We must continue to love them, guide them and weigh our decisions against their need to grow independently. We can help them process and make sense of the world around them. We need to help them early on to navigate the world with as many coping skills as possible. These skills are critical whether your baby is two, twelve, or twenty-two years old. The guiding question of "Will it matter in ten years?"

can help to be a guiding framework throughout their lives so they can start looking at their own behaviors and decisions with a longer term concept in mind.

I will say it again. The rewards of raising a great kid are immeasurable. To take a step back and see a young adult who is respectful and kind, reaches out to others in an honest manner, who can patiently wait and persevere toward a successful role in the world is amazing. To see this same person take on responsibilities for himself and others and to make wise decisions is awesome. To see this person be socially capable and live up to their commitments and put safe limits on themselves is a dream. To know that we helped guide him there produces an overwhelming feeling of pride and love. It is the greatest success we can have as a parent.

The bottom line is, as we juggle life in a hectic and busy way, taking in all the information we can about our children and their world, we need to continue to ask ourselves, "Will it matter in ten years?" Every time we ask ourselves this question we reinforce our commitment to raising responsible and respectful young adults who will be fully capable of coping within our societal expectations. The time, energy, and commitment on our part are so worth it. The short-term battles for the long-term benefits are so worth it. The parenting decisions we make and the actions we take now are important and will impact our children in both tangible and intangible ways. Our critical actions or inactions will tip the scales one way or another as we make daily decisions while raising your children.

What kind of adolescent do you want in ten years? The choice really is yours. Paying attention to your parenting decisions really is worth it at every step in your child's journey to adulthood. Enjoy the journey. The ten years will fly by!

The following are suggested readings I have enjoyed that you may also enjoy, while raising your children. From some of these I have learned a tremendous amount; some have made me stop and reflect quite a bit. Some of these just help to keep life in perspective.

Bolman, L. & Deal, T. (2001). *Leading with Soul: An Uncommon Journey of Spirit (new & revised)*. Jossey Bass, CA.

Bradley, M. (2001). *Yes, Your Teen Is Crazy: Loving Your Kid without Losing Your Mind*. Harbor Press, Washington.

Giannetti, C. & Sagarese, M. (2001). *Cliques: 8 Steps to Helping Your Child Survive the Social Jungle*. Broadway Books: Random House, New York, NY.

Gurian, M. (2002). *The Wonder of Girls: Understanding the Hidden Nature of Our Daughters*. Atria Books, NY.

Niven, D. (2002). The *100 Simple Secrets of Successful People*. Harper Collins Publisher; New York, NY.

Pearson, A. (2002). *I Don't Know How She Does It*. Alfred A. Knopf, NY.

Pay It Forward—Great movie to help adolescents see how their actions can impact those around them in powerful ways. Watch it with them. It is wonderful.

Simmons, R. (2002). *Odd Girl Out: The Hidden Culture of Aggression in Girls*. Harcourt Books, FL.

Tarbox, K. (2001). *Katie.com: My Story*. Penguin-Putnam Books, NY.

0-595-31638-7

Printed in the United States
23210LVS00007B/235-288

9 780595 316380